D1711268

THE WAY THEY SHOULD GO

The Way
They Should Go

D. BRUCE LOCKERBIE

New York
OXFORD UNIVERSITY PRESS
1972

Acknowledgments

Many people gave generously of their time and vigor to help me in writing this book.

Both the Headmaster Emeritus, Dr. Frank E. Gaebelein, and the present headmaster, Donn M. Gaebelein, offered without restriction the resources of their experience at The Stony Brook School. The records of the School and their correspondence were available to me; when clarification or insight was needed, I benefited from lengthy and candid interviews. At no point, however, did either man attempt to influence the opinions being put forward in the final shaping of this book.

I profited immeasurably from the careful reading given parts of the manuscript by three friends and mentors: Pierson Curtis, retired senior master, whose forty-four years at Stony Brook gave him the broadest available view of the School; Dr. J. Wesley Ingles, whose experience as a former teacher at Stony Brook and as a distinguished writer equipped him doubly as my consultant and critic; and Dr. Clyde S. Kilby, whose scholarly gifts have always transmitted themselves to me in paternal affection.

Dr. John F. Blanchard, Jr., executive director of the National Association of Christian Schools, Dr. Harold John Ockenga, president of Gordon College and Gordon-Conwell Theological Seminary, and Dr. William L. Pressly, president of The Westminster Schools, Atlanta, Georgia, provided me with factual information.

Mrs. Clacia Young supplied invaluable aid by collecting and evaluating documents for research. Mrs. Elizabeth Murray and Mrs. Lois Stokey performed innumerable clerical tasks willingly and efficiently. Mrs. Mary Rost typed and proofread the final manuscript.

An anonymous donor, an alumnus of The Stony Brook School, contributed a grant which made possible the fulfillment of this project. Many other alumni cooperated by furnishing me with their observations on the experience and education they had received at Stony Brook.

To all these people, both individually and collectively, my deep expression of gratitude.

This book bears no dedication. Rather, I wish to acknowledge the debt I feel to my colleagues who by their faithful stewardship as Christian teachers gave encouragement to my work.

No mere phrase encompasses the realization I have that I owe my greatest appreciation to my wife Lory.

Preface

Walt Whitman would scarcely recognize most of his beloved "fish-shap'd Paumanok" today. Criss-crossed by vast strips of concrete, harvesting acres of three-bedroom bungalows where farmers once reaped Long Island spuds, the fifty miles from New York City to Stony Brook is a kaleidoscope of the megalopolis. A few minutes out of the tunnel under the East River brings the traveler to Scott Fitzgerald's "valley of ashes," the site of two world's fairs. Across the boundary separating the Borough of Queens from Nassau County, you pass, on one side, the manorial homes of the nameless rich and, on the other, Levittown.

But as the road sweeps into Suffolk County, the terrain to the north rises sharply from the flatness of a glacial plain. Now scrubby, sand-stunted trees change to great oaks and elms; dogwood, mountain laurel, and rhododendron grow in profusion. The countryside is rolling and lush, suggesting what Fitzgerald may have meant when he imagined the first reaction of the Dutch explorers to this "fresh, green breast of the new world."

Arriving at Stony Brook, the visitor finds both the new and the old. The community's respect for antiquity preserves much of the natural appeal through its zoning laws, its museums and landmarks, its authentic Early American festival. For what has already been lost, the rehabilitated village center, constructed in the design of the Federal period, presents an ersatz reminder.

Still the old has not withstood the new. Here are both the mass-produced development house and the 200-year-old saltbox; an artist's "happening" and the work of a nineteenth-century American master; a sparkling marina and remains of an important shipbuilding industry of 150 years ago; a Bohack supermarket and the village grist mill operating since 1699; at the roadside an abandoned Chevrolet and in the Carriage Museum an Italian gig dating back to 1695.

Here too are visible reminders of the schism in another phase of American life—the education of youth. Two institutions represent the differences between education that is state-controlled and secular and education choosing to be independent and Christian in its teaching. On opposite sides of the Long Island Railroad tracks stand a branch of the State University of New York and The Stony Brook School. The State University espouses an education that is essentially man-centered. The depth of secularism at the university may be suggested by the observation that its principal courses in religious thought are taught by a leading death-of-God theologian. The Stony Brook School, on the other hand, accepts as its premise man's need for a relationship with God and the abiding truth of God's revelation through Jesus Christ and the written Word.

Religion in the schools is no anomaly to American life. Its roots go deep into American history. The first schools founded here—at Saint Augustine in 1606, at Boston in 1635, at New Amsterdam in 1638—were established to educate both the mind and soul by inculcating religious truths. Long into the years of the Republic these same objectives remained important, even after the emergence of universal public education. But democratizing pressures and increasingly secular attitudes eventually ousted the teaching of religion from the public classrooms. Even some of the old private schools allowed the teaching of religion, and of Christian doctrine, in particular, to wane. In time, the original purposes of American education had been virtually eradicated from all but a few remaining schools.

That such schools should exist at all, of course, is a phenomenon of American democracy not found in many other countries. Here a family may choose the form and nature of its children's schooling. According to *A Study of the American Independent School,* "one student in every eight throughout the nation attends a nonpublic school." True, this fact alone is galling to the extreme egalitarian, who regards the parent's right as an elitist an undemocratic fly in the ointment. Still the right exists, "a natural concomitant of a pluralistic society," the *Study* declares, reaffirmed by the 1925 Supreme Court decision regarding private schooling in Oregon.

In this matter of free choice, both schools and parents are also able to establish an environment in which a particular religious preference might flourish; parents may place their offspring in such an environment. Schools wishing to declare and maintain a religious—or political or cultural—point of view are free to formulate a philosophy of education that expresses the manner of life articulated in their creeds and confessions. The purpose of such a philosophy is, in general, to convey to young minds the peculiar efficacy of shaping one's life around the central core of truth, as they see it. Of course, no one is compelled to attend such a school; it must win its own constituency.

The American independent school has this right—indeed, this obligation—to express itself differently from the pluralism of the public schools. If it does not, the nonpublic school abrogates its own authority, disenfranchises itself as an *independent* institution, and falls easily into the class of mere proprietary corporations.

Among independent schools are some whose philosophy expresses a Christian faith. By far the largest segment of these schools belongs to the Roman Catholic Church; among the Protestant denominations, the Episcopal and various Lutheran affiliations sponsor some 2000 schools. Other denominations active in the Christian school movement are the Christian Reformed Church and the Seventh-Day Adventists.

There are also Christian schools operating without direct connection to any denomination. Two federations claim almost 700 such schools in the United States, Canada, and overseas. The National Union of Christian Schools retains close national and theological ties with Dutch and Reformational traditions; the National Association of Christian Schools attempts to correlate the strength and influence of interdenominational, evangelical schools.

Many of these evangelical schools are small and struggling. Many do not have their own buildings and meet in the facilities of cooperating churches. Others have grown to splendid campuses and sturdy reputations. Only a few, however, like The Stony Brook School, are boarding schools, following in the tradition of Vittorino da Feltre, whose "House of Joy" in Mantua was the first boarding school. There this fifteenth-century teacher sought to imbue his students with the wholeness of a Christian humanistic education by providing a Christian example in a residential situation.

Stony Brook takes as its motto "Character before Career," asserting that Christian character, which stems from a personal relationship with God through Christ, must take priority over any secular or material concern. The phrase sums up Stony Brook's reason for being—the purpose of every truly Christian school. Philips Packer Eliot refers to the motto in his exposition of The Book of Judges, in *The Interpreter's Bible*. Speaking of men like Samson who abuse power given them, Eliot says,

> With such power given to the individual, it is more important than ever that we should develop men and women of integrity. The slogan of The Stony Brook School on Long Island is "Character before Career." It is utterly unabashed in thus placing goodness before success. Power is good if the man is good who wields it. In foreign affairs we need not simply "career" diplomats; we need "character" diplomats and we need them first.

Aiming so high, the Christian school must also be aware that it often falls short of providing either the intellectual stimulus or Christian nurture necessary for establishing character. Thus this book does not claim the unqualified success of Christian education as practiced at Stony Brook or anywhere else. It is an account of what can happen when Christian education is permitted as an alternative to secularism. The final assessment of such a program is entrusted, as John Amos Comenius said, to "the care of the Eternal Teacher, the Holy Spirit."

I have written this book, admittedly, from the vantage of an insider, one who knows well The Stony Brook School and its approach to Christian education. I have spent fifteen years as teacher and coach, as dormitory resident and counselor. I have seen my three children grow to an age when they too are now enrolled at Stony Brook. Yet I hope the reader will find that this book is more than a narrow, self-congratulatory tribute to a single school. Stony Brook is a small school with a short history (it was founded in 1922) and a comparatively small constituency. While size is not always a measure of significance, an intimate detailing of Stony Brook's first fifty years would have only limited value—and to an audience already sentimentally attached to the School.

But the story of Christian education is old, noble in tradition, deserving of a wider audience. The purpose of this book is to tell something of that tradition, identifying the contribution of one

Christian school among many. Thereby I hope to encourage the support of Christian schools—at Stony Brook and wherever men and women are willing to join together to train young people in the fear and admonition of the Lord.

When Stony Brook was still a new school, its young headmaster, Frank E. Gaebelein, wrote,

The existence of this school has a significance far beyond its size. It is a pioneer. Great as its individual work is, its mission of blazing the way for other schools to follow in its path is even greater. Indeed it is the earnest hope of its founders that the success of The Stony Brook School will stimulate the organization of many another institution of similar aims and ideals. There cannot be too many such.

Stony Brook, New York   D. B. L.
1972

Contents

THE WAY THEY SHOULD GO

1

A Christian Alternative

American education careens from generation to generation, supported at times by a heady idealism, at other times by financial expediency. We have passed from a period of optimism into the latter stages of widespread distress over the state of our schools. Across the nation local communities are experiencing the discontent of parents and taxpayers as school boards are overturned and school budgets voted down. Everywhere the cries are for reform. Everywhere one hears talk about "free schools," "open schools," "open corridors," "flexible scheduling," and "individualized instruction packages." Everywhere the search is on for a new method, a fresh pedagogy, because, as Charles Silberman says in *Crisis in the Classroom,* "Ours is an age of crisis."

Uniformly, writers on education in America recognize the symptoms of the problem; they are too apparent to be ignored. These symptoms range from reading inefficiency throughout whole schools to intellectual malaise among graduate students in selective universities. They manifest themselves in parental outrage and in armed encounters between undergraduates and the National Guard. But these, we point out again, are only symptoms of the problem. Treating any or all of them does nothing to eliminate the problem itself, for the problem in today's education is, at root, the problem with today's society: It is glutted with its own secularism.

The ferment among our youth results from their rejection of adult mores. They refuse to become, in Theodore Roszak's terms, "technocracy's children" and prefer to unite in "the making of a counter culture." So the flight from one world of home, school, business, and perhaps church to another world—a new Eden, a new Atlantis, ruled by the single standard of love.

In some extreme cases, where immaturity has led them to discard all semblance of their parents' manner of living, these youth refuse to discriminate between causes and effects. If the object or action has upon it the stench of customary adult usage, it is abandoned. As Ada Louise Huxtable of *The New York Times*, observes in an interview, "Young people are dropping out of a society that we have built; they're dropping out of suburbia and the developer's house with a two-car garage; they're dropping out of everything that their parents thought was the ideal environment."

In other cases, rejection by the young expresses itself in attitude rather than in overt action. While remaining within the perimeter of conventional society—whether because of timidity or inertia—these youths are nonetheless as opposed to the values maintained by the adult generation as are their dropout peers. They too have no intention of following the patterns laid out for them by parents, teachers, clergy, and bureaucrats. They hint at their rebelliousness in their music and modish dress, but a better gauge may be their vocational aimlessness. We live at a time when an Ivy League graduate may profess that driving a metropolitan taxicab is his highest vocational goal. Young men and women now find it respectable to live off unemployment benefits or the public dole.

This diagrams the crisis in education. Young people are not saying, "Change the methods by which you teach" but "Change what you teach." Change the schools by changing the value structure on which those schools are based—a foundation of democratic platitudes ("All men are created equal"), pseudo-religious mouthings ("the value of the individual"), and free enterprise slogans ("Unicard, Unicard, so you don't have to settle for second best"). Change the mindless pretense of impartiality on all issues of importance and take a position. Become a real person; see others as persons. Believe in something enough to be willing to die for it; more important, be willing to live for it.

The restoration of personal values is what today's youth seek. They want to become, as Paul Tournier puts it, "whole persons in a broken world." Even the Port Huron Statement, issued in 1962 by Students for a Democratic Society, cannot be ignored in spite of subsequent violence committed in the name of SDS. It said, in part,

We regard *men* as infinitely precious and possessed of unfulfilled capacities for reason, freedom, and love. . . . We oppose the depersonalization that reduces human beings to the status of things. . . . Loneliness, estrangement, isolation describe the vast distances between man and man today.

If these sentiments were sincere, then Paul Goodman is accurate in considering student protest as "a religious crisis of the magnitude of the Reformation in the fifteen-hundreds." That too was a shaking off of the old order, characterized by a rejection of established religion and a return to the ideal of personal relationships as found in early Christianity.

The liberal churchman William Stringfellow sees the crisis in similar terms. Addressing the Council for Religion in Independent Schools, he says, "So let none be astonished or unduly distressed by crisis nowadays. Of course there is crisis: crisis is the normative human situation, empirically, historically, and biblically. Crisis, far from being some novel, occasional or recent occurrence is, in truth, a synonym for the Fall."

Stringfellow thus connects the present crisis to the innate spiritual condition of man. One cannot doubt that a sense of this condition is responsible for the religious phenomenon known as "the Jesus Movement." It is part of the whole youthful search for what sociologists call "alternative structures." These young people have tried and forsaken their parents' ways after finding only conformity and suffocation. They have tried and abandoned the vacuum of the street or the commune with its diet of drugs and death. They have caught a glimpse of Satanism and its effects upon a Charles Manson. In their quest for life they have found that the Person of Jesus provides both the end and the means to attain it.

If educational decisions reflect one's philosophy of life, then the reason American society in general and education in particular has been giving its youth the wrong answer is that we have been proponents of the wrong philosophy. But most commentators on American society would agree with the playwright Arthur Miller's statement that "there is not among us any commonly accepted faith in a way of life that will give us not only material gain but satisfaction."

We need to find such a faith; unless we do, we stand in danger not of crisis but chaos. I believe we need to restore the Christian alternative to secular education.

Silberman and other critics have blamed "the schools"—by

which they mean both the buildings and those within them—and they call loudly for reform. But when Silberman cites the work of John Amos Comenius, the seventeenth-century scholar and writer, as a model reformer, he does not tell his readers that Comenius was more than "a religious reformer . . . concerned with the moral instruction of the young." The reader never learns that Comenius was, in fact, a bishop among the Moravian Christians who called themselves the Unity of Brethren; that he was a political exile because of his zealous Christian faith; that he was invited to become president of Harvard College and to take his part in "a plan for the propagation of the Gospel among the heathen" (meaning New England's Indian tribes); that he was, in short, an evangelical Christian whose reforms in education, especially as presented in *The Great Didactic* (1627-32), from which Silberman quotes repeatedly, were for the purpose of strengthening a child's personal experience through faith in Jesus Christ.

The man hailed as "the founder of modern educational theory" would be perplexed today by the way his theories have been applied. For while Comenius urged the opportunity of education for all, he would have condemned the present dilution of moral principles into a tepid tolerance of atheistic, satanistic, and theistic views alike. While Comenius knew firsthand the anguish of religious persecution (in 1621, he was cut off from his wife and children by having to flee Spanish invaders), he would not approve the exclusion of the Bible from American public schools. His biographer, Matthew Spinka, in *That Incomparable Moravian,* speaks of "the strong biblical emphasis . . . reflected in Comenius' elevation of the Bible to the place of supreme authority as the norm of all knowledge." Spinka continues, "To this view he remained faithful throughout his life, and it is reflected in all his writings." Strange, is it not, that present admirers of Comenius among both educators and their critics should ignore the base from which the great Moravian wrote?

Yet not so strange, for many of these educators and critics are but themselves the products of secularized education which has cut itself off from its historic roots in Christian truth. Was not William Butler Yeats speaking of our age when he wrote, in "The Second Coming,"

Turning and turning in the widening gyre,
The falcon cannot hear the falconer;
Things fall apart, the centre cannot hold.

At one time our society had a central fixed point of reference for our moral values—what Dean Calvin Linton of George Washington University calls "the motionless center." Radiating outward, spiraling upward from society's common knowledge of the Scriptures went the issues of life—the vocation of men; their search for truth, beauty, and goodness in the arts and in nature; and the yearning for God. Men might journey and men might climb, but always the permanent center of things remained for men to return to.

In the ages of man's development he has mastered the wheel and rudder; he has invented the alphabet and the twelve-tone scale; he has raised his boundary to the moon and now looks beyond. Yet he has not mastered himself, and so "things fall apart." Lacking a focus of meaning, he finds that "the centre cannot hold." Abandoned to his own ethical relativism, he finds himself, like Melville's Ishmael, stabbed from behind with the thought of his own annihilation.

What is true of life in general is also true of much of education in particular. The "spiral curriculum" proposed by Jerome Bruner has been a valuable addition to educational theory. But a spiral that loses contact with its base becomes only a spinning rotary, twisting catastrophically into dizziness. The teacher who rides such a spiral will find himself, like the Islamic dervish, whirling and howling himself into oblivion. I speak, of course, of the spiral that winds away from the very roots of learning, man's search for answers to the fundamental questions of his soul: Who am I? Where did I come from? Where am I going? To these questions secular education has no reply.

In the backwash of court decisions regarding public education, administrative edicts from frightened superintendents and school boards, pressured by intolerant dissidents, seem bent on demonstrating their enlightened disinterestedness in religion. They are so secular minded that *both* the nativity scene and the menorah have been forbidden, as though they were without cultural value. In most public schools the literary power and ethical influence of the English Bible are lost to students, a fact the National Council of Teachers of English laments and seeks to correct by sponsoring a workshop on teaching the Bible. In a pose of objectivity many schools offer their students not the power of conviction but merely the paralysis of convention.

In his personal narrative, *A Walker in the City,* Alfred Kazin recalls the importance placed upon *character* in his Brooklyn schooling. In his childish uncertainty, one thing was sure:

> Character belonged to great adults. Yet we were constantly being driven onto it; it was the great threshold we had to cross.

Only through the demonstration of "satisfactory marks of character" could the New York City schoolboy receive his diploma. Now, by a decision of Chancellor Harvey Scribner, the New York City public schools have removed the requirement that behavior and citizenship be weighed in the awarding of a high school diploma.

Baseless, rootless, its historic connections to the values of Judaism and Christianity cut, much of American education revolves like a burned-out satellite. Regrettably, some professed religionists themselves have assisted in severing American education from its traditional ties with a religious heritage. "Modern biblical science," writes Spinka, "has not approved Comenius' implicit faith in the Bible." Instead some theologians, disdainful of the Scriptures as revealed truth, have adopted political or social theories as their maxims for moral improvement. Consciously or not, such theologians have joined with educators in devitalizing American education by draining its religious character and substituting raw secularism.

Thus, commenting on the failure of schools and colleges with Protestant affiliation to remain loyal to their traditional goals, William Arrowsmith has said, "The result is the irrelevance, even hypocrisy that students so rightfully protest: . . . institutions with ecumenical traditions subverted into serving as mere instruments of national purpose; church-related colleges and universities junking the traditions that make them different and educationally unique in the effort to achieve an undistinguished secular modernity."

Silberman, Goodman, and other philosophically minded critics of education see that the problem is far greater than we had heretofore supposed. "Our most pressing educational problem," says Silberman, "is not how to increase the efficiency of the schools; it is how to create and maintain a humane society." Yet a humane society can never be derived from a secular matrix, for secularism, with its emphasis upon things as opposed to persons, lacks humaneness and human concern. According to Jacques Ellul's forecast in *The Technological Society,* the secular dystopia of the future is "a future Huxley never dreamed of." At its worst, secularism is responsible for the effectiveness of Belsen's "final solution" and the debauchery of a Forty-second Street peep show. Indeed, even now the language by which conventional morality expresses itself no longer seems appropriate in a context of secularism; somehow it seems outdated to our sophisticated ears. The film critic, Richard Schickel, writing in *Life* magazine, spoke to this point:

> I am compelled to note one curiosity in the responses of the audience with whom I saw the film [*The Blue Max*]. Whenever an aristocrat drew himself up to define the old-fashioned code of honor, he was immediately drowned out by giggles and guffaws. Perhaps crudeness in acting or direction accounted for this reaction, but not all of it. We are now so far gone in moral ambiguity and so drunk on the spirit of camp that the old verities may not be mentioned without drawing laughter.

Still, in spite of the crisis facing educators and parents of children to be educated, there is and always has been a solution available to those who wish it. The American tradition of freedom of choice in education has preserved the American independent schools and among them the Christian schools practicing Christian education. William G. Saltonstall, former principal of Phillips' Exeter Academy, has written:

> Perhaps the most cherished freedom of the independent school is the freedom to include the teaching of religious and ethical values within the formalized structure of the curriculum.

This is certainly true, and many private schools exert their prerogative by conducting classes in ethics or in comparative religion or in sacred studies, mindful, as the British philosopher and mathematician Alfred North Whitehead contended, that "the essence of education is that it be religious." Such programs of study, however, do not in themselves comprise what one means by Christian education.

"Christian education," the neo-orthodox theologian Joseph Haroutunian acknowledges, "means education according to the Christian faith." James Kallas offers this definition: *"Christian* education is the impartation of a point of view that puts Christ at that vital integrative center, that insists it is with him as Alpha and Omega that all human history and knowledge is to be comprehended." Accordingly, Christian education is "a deliberate attempt to cultivate the conviction that it is not only proper and legitimate but also vitally necessary to see all things from the vantage point of the Cross." To Calvin Seerveld, Christian education is education "where there is a conscious, willed, obviously concerted effort to proclaim in all its scandalous intolerance that the mind of Jesus Christ is the only true way for life and knowledge, in biology, history, literature, geography."

In short, Christian education takes as its view of the world the assumption, in St. Paul's words, that "God was in Christ reconciling the world unto himself." It is education that shares Comenius' concern, expressed in *The Great Didactic:*

> The first care, therefore, ought to be of the soul, which is the principal part of the man, so that it may become, in the highest degree possible, beautifully adorned. The next care is for the body, that it may be made a habitation fit and worthy of an immortal soul. Regard the mind as rightly instructed which is truly illuminated from the effulgence of the wisdom of God, so that man, contemplating the presence of the Divine Image in himself, may diligently observe and guard that excellence.

Beyond Comenius, however, stands an even higher model for the Christian educator. The evangelist Luke records that the boy Jesus "increased in wisdom and in stature, and in favor with God and man." The Christian educator must offer training for the mind and body; he must prepare his students for their responsibilities in society. But he must also point them to their need to find favor with God. This he will do by example as well as by direct teaching. His aim in so doing will always be to lead his students and himself in inquiring after the two ultimate questions asked long ago by St. Paul: "Who art thou, Lord?" and "Lord, what wilt thou have me to do?"

There is nothing new about the Christian alternative in education. Its roots go as deep as the Early Church and the teaching given to Timothy by his mother and grandmother. In Europe and throughout the New World the Christian schoolmaster brought with him the first amenities of civilization. Education as we know it in America is the direct offspring of the Christian Church.

* * *

For the greater part of our history, American education and Christian education were synonymous terms. John Harvard's bequest founded Harvard College in 1636 so that the Massachusetts Bay Colony might not suffer "an illiterate Ministry to the Churches, when our present Ministers shall lie in the Dust." The founding charter of every colonial college thereafter, except the College of Philadelphia (now the University of Pennsylvania), expressed its intention to prepare young men for the Gospel ministry.

Along with Harvard College, seven other colleges were begun by Christian educators before the Revolutionary War. Yale College (1701) and Dartmouth College (1769) were established, like Harvard, by Congregationalists. The College of William and Mary (1693) and Columbia College (King's College, 1754) were sponsored by the Church of England. Princeton (1746), then called the College of New Jersey, was founded by Presbyterians; Brown (1764), first known as Rhode Island College, by Baptists; Rutgers (1766), by the Dutch Reformed Church.

This trend continued in the new Republic. Amherst College, to name only one, was founded in 1821 and dedicated to "the education of indigent young men of piety and talents for the Christian ministry." At about the same time, Presbyterians in Kentucky were opening their new institution, Centre College, hoping there to maintain a spiritual bulwark against the power of an encroaching secularism.

This incursion of secularism is, of course, the theme of the transition, both politically and spiritually, from a colonial theocracy to the American democracy. In its most clearly defined state, the theocracy of New England had proposed a colony of saints pursuing its divine "errand into the wilderness." The Massachusetts Bay Colony had adopted as its official seal the figure of an American Indian speaking the words of St. Paul's apostolic vision, "Come over into Macedonia and help us" (Acts 16:9). Its official spokesmen, the clergymen and successive governors, looked upon Puritan society as a fulfillment of the Macedonian call.

The Puritan oligarchy well knew, however, that training of the clergy and other acknowledged leaders must begin with the education of children. They agreed with Luther, who, in 1530, had preached a sermon entitled "On the Duty of Sending Children to School." Literacy was the first step toward an understanding of the Scriptures; instruction of the young by their elders was part of Christian vocation. One year before the founding of Harvard College, therefore, Boston Latin School had been opened, patterned after English grammar schools such as St. Paul's and Winchester with which its founders were familiar. Soon neighboring towns established their own schools. In Roxbury, for example, Governor Thomas Dudley and the Reverend John Eliot, the famous "Apostle to the Indians," were among the forty-four who signed their names to the school's 1645 charter.

In 1647, the Massachusetts legislature passed an education act stipulating that towns of fifty or more families must appoint and support a teacher of reading and writing, thereby establishing the "common school" in America. Towns of one hundred or more families must provide a Latin teacher whose responsibility was the preparation of boys for admission to Harvard College. In cases where schools were not established, parents were nonetheless responsible for teaching their children well enough "to read and understand the principles of religion and the capital laws of the country," the statute said. The prototype for a public school system in America, therefore, was community-controlled, yet it emphasized a direct connection with the religious faith of its constituents.

The original purpose of education as established in New England was closely tied to the preservation of Christian orthodoxy; understandably, the earliest teachers were also ordained ministers. Not until 1738 did Harvard College permit a layman, John Winthrop, to teach science.

The standard curriculum at Harvard consisted of classical languages to aid the study of the Scriptures, natural philosophy or science with which to prove the wonder-workings of God's creation, and theology by which to codify and test a man's faith. Likewise, in both the common and the Latin schools, learning was grounded upon the rote recitation of Puritan verities. Children learned the alphabet from *The New England Primer* (1683), a series of mnemonic rhymes tracing Bible stories from A to Z:

> *In Adam's fall*
> *We sinned all.*
>
> *Zaccheus he*
> *Did climb a tree*
> *Our Lord to see.*

The Bible, the Apostles' Creed, and a catechism called "Spiritual Milk for American Babes" supplied literature for reading. At about the time that the English Separatists were removing themselves to Holland, the colony of Virginia was already passing through the struggles of its first year. Yet it was not until more than eighty years had passed, in 1692, that repeated attempts to begin a college in the colony resulted in a charter for the College of William and Mary, opened the following year. As early as 1619, such an institution had been planned for Henrico; as in New England, however, the exigencies of colonial life—in particular, the ravages of Indian attacks—made it necessary to divert funds for survival purposes.

The Virginians differed substantially from the Puritans to the north. Essentially aristocratic in their class consciousness, the Virginia community had transplanted its English traditions to America. It was not expected that education should be provided for all. Landowners could well afford to send their sons to schools across the Atlantic. For those who chose to keep their young men at home, some few Latin schools provided the necessary preparation for the English universities. Clergymen offered instruction in the catechism; apprentices were given rudimentary training by their masters. But although the Virginia legislature passed a resolution in 1660 calling for "a free school for the advancement of learning, education of youth, supply of the ministry, and promotion of piety," Virginia offered little more, in fact, than home training by literate parents. Moreover, there was opposition in high places to the establishment of a free school system. Governor William Berkeley expressed his thanks to God that "there are no free schools, and I hope we shall not have them these hundred years; for learning has brought disobedience and heresy and sects into the world."

Throughout the rest of Colonial America, the attitude was much the same, except in New Netherlands, Pennsylvania, and, as noted, in Massachusetts. The Dutch Reformed Church, under the auspices of the Classis of Amsterdam, founded the Collegiate School in 1638 in New Amsterdam, now New York. Among the Dutch, the parochial school, whose founding accompanied almost every church, reflected the insistence of Calvin and other reformers upon education for all. Yet Dutch political authorities provided no statutory requirements for such schools, as did the Massachusetts legislators. Instead Dutch schools sprang from the conviction, expressed by the Synod of Dort in 1618, that education was a necessity for every Christian.

In Pennsylvania, the Quakers also practiced a system that called for the establishing of a school with every meetinghouse. In 1689, the Friends' Select School and the school now known as the William Penn Charter School were founded in Philadelphia. By 1701, the Pennsylvania legislature had granted a charter, signed by William Penn, which resulted in the development of a number of elementary schools. This act also encouraged the founding of similar secondary schools such as the Abington Friends' School begun in 1697.

The Quakers' characteristic tolerance of all creeds attracted Lutherans, Moravians, and Mennonites to establish schools in Pennsylvania to perpetuate their social and religious customs. By the mid-eighteenth century, Bethlehem and Lititz were Moravian educational centers, and at Neshaminy, William Tennent's "Log College," a Presbyterian theological seminary in the wilderness, was producing fiery revivalists.

Meanwhile in Philadelphia itself, Benjamin Franklin had founded a nonsectarian academy. In his view, freedom *of* religion and freedom *from* religion were not antithetical. Franklin's intention as an educator was to keep his academy undenominational and therefore open to free inquiry. As an expression of his own breadth of mind, Franklin invited the visiting English evangelist George Whitefield to preach at his academy.

In Maryland, similar examples of religious tolerance had been demonstrated by the Roman Catholic Calvert family, the first Lord Baltimore and his sons who succeeded him as hereditary possessors of the royal colony. But formal education was not available in Maryland until after 1677, when a Jesuit school was founded.

Throughout the American colonies, then, the pervasive influences of the organized Christian church monopolized attempts at popular education. With the exception of Franklin's academy and later college, no institution recognized the possibility of a wholly secular education; nowhere but in Philadelphia was it admissible to consider obtaining an education outside the Christian frame of reference.

In spite of this, even the most militantly religious colonies were unable to prevent the incursions of secularism. The purging trials in Massachusetts, which sent Roger Williams and Mistress Anne Hutchinson into exile, rooted out some forms of religious dissent; later, the Salem witch trials of 1692 would dramatize the Puritan zeal in exorcising sin. But none of these measures could fully contend with outright unbelief and secular concerns. Moreover, as the early educators soon discovered, the rigors of the wilderness required a knowledge of the "useful arts" as well as stimulation for the life of the mind and spirit.

The dispersion of the population from original settlements along the Atlantic coast affected the curriculum in the schools that grew out of the frontier experience. For the most part, settlers on the wilderness's edge did not carry with them the same concern for a classical education that had motivated the founders of the Latin schools and Harvard College. As Rush Welter points out in his book, *Popular Education and Democratic Thought in America,* "the depredations and the financial burdens of Indian wars" were among the forces destructive of the early priority given to formal schooling. Welter writes:

> As the first well-educated generation died, as the population spread out in ever greater diffusion, as the original religious impulse waned and was replaced by an urgent quest for prosperity, and as the clergy lost first their political and then their religious monopoly, the common schools fared badly and the Latin schools fared worse.

More and more the practice—for there could be no system as such defined—of education in frontier America reverted to the old English tradition: schooling in the home from literate parents and apprenticeship to a trade. If his parents were incapable of teaching, the child might be sent to a widow who supported herself by conducting a "dame school," in which reading and writing were taught; more often, illiterate parents perpetuated an illiterate progeny. And where there was no faith in the home, the benefits of religious instruction were lost altogether, for it was invariably true that communities without schools were also without churches—they were *hamlets* in the strictest sense of the word. The "Great Awakening" of the 1730s somewhat alleviated this situation by restoring, through a spiritual revival, at least enough concern for literacy to enable reading of the Scriptures. But it also worked ironically to the disadvantage of a genuine American education because out of the revivals of that period came a profound spirit of anti-intellectualism, in spite of the fact that many of the principal evangelists were themselves learned men. To be sure, some colleges grew directly out of the religious ecstasy—the "Log College," for instance—but they were not founded to augment the education offered at Harvard, William and Mary, or Yale, but to oppose it. Jonathan Edwards, for example, expressed the attitude of the Awakened toward scholars of the Enlightenment at Harvard and Yale, accusing them of failing to be "nurseries of piety," more interested in teaching "the scholars human learning" than in indoctrinating them in the faith.

By this point, therefore, a reversal of attitudes toward education for the common man had developed. Initially regarded as the handmaiden of the Church, education was now widely scoffed at as a frippery, if not an outright subversion by the Devil. In the later colonial period, through the French-Indian War, and on to the War of Independence, illiteracy increased; so, too, did indifference toward religion. Thus, one discovers an essential paradox in American social history: when religion rejected education, a consequential ignorance rejected religion.

In the sophisticated centers of civilization, those who still respected the human intellect and honored reason above their emotions were easily put off by the radicalism of the revivalists. Turning to the writings of French and German philosophy, they drifted into the comfortable doctrines of deism and pantheism. Gradually their influence placed them in positions of leadership in the churches and schools of New England. By the early 1800s, the Harvard Divinity School had become a Unitarian seminary; by 1838, Ralph Waldo Emerson, himself a graduate of the School and an ordained Unitarian pastor until he demitted the ministry, was addressing the graduating class and telling them that any suggestion that Jesus was uniquely divine was a "noxious doctrine."

* * *

Throughout the nineteenth century, American education grew increasingly secular and antagonistic toward its roots in orthodox Christianity. The rise of the public schools, established first in Massachusetts under Horace Mann in 1837, created a new environment for education. In the burgeoning American democracy, the melting pot theory of social adaptation required a nonsectarian approach to whatever moral instruction was offered. When Mann suggested that Bible reading be included in public education, some Christians cheered; others attacked Mann and his proposal on two grounds: first, that Christian doctrine would become diluted in the hands of secular-minded teachers, and, second, that Protestantism would lose ground to the increasing number of Catholic immigrants.

In this latter regard, the loudest advocates of Christian orthodoxy were unable to recognize that, in a changing democratic state, an egalitarian approach to religious instruction must be maintained in any public school. Some of these militant Christians would not stop short of demanding—and in some cases obtaining—legislation that required the daily reading of the King James Version of the Bible to the exclusion of any other version, a direct affront to the Catholic position at that time. But in 1853, Horace Bushnell, a liberal theologian and pastor in Hartford, and the author of an important book on the teaching of youth called *Christian Nurture,* argued for schools, even if Christian doctrine could not be a part of their curriculum. Bushnell recognized the priority of education in a pluralistic society, which distinguishes him from many of his Christian contemporaries. Their narrowness would have preferred a universal ignorance over a system of education that did not propagate the truth precisely as they understood it. Not surprisingly, this same narrowness led some branches of the church into a rejection of formal learning similar to the reactionary anti-intellectualism during and after the "Great Awakening" a century before.

This reactionary spirit coincided with the rise of the "Know Nothing" party in America, also called the "Native American" movement. Among its tenets was outright anti-Roman Catholic bigotry, veiled behind proposals for immigration and residency requirements. Many Protestant evangelicals aligned themselves with this movement, not unlike the participation of some similar Protestant groups in racist organizations now. Then, as now, they wished the school to be a haven of protection against the outside world, rather than a place of preparation for young people learning how to encounter the world.

The exceptions to this rule were those Christians who were also ardently persuaded that slavery should be abolished. In the years leading to midcentury, several groups of Eastern-educated opponents of slavery founded Christian schools and colleges in the states and territories of the Northwest. They hoped that a double influence of the Christian gospel and enlightenment of education might preserve the West from the infection of slavery.

The effects of the Civil War and industrialization forced a revision of attitudes toward education by many who had previously been indifferent. Most European immigrants saw that only through the education of their children could Americanization be realized. Farmers who had taken no strong position regarding universal education now banded together under the National Grange of the Patrons of Husbandry to ensure adequate schooling for rural families. Negroes deprived of education before Emancipation now sought opportunities to learn. Most of the sustaining opportunities came from the Christian benevolence of denominational groups, forming Freedmen's Societies out of which grew church-sponsored schools and seminaries, such as the Richmond Theological School for Freedmen (1865), now Virginia Union University.

But the aftermath of war and the growth of urban industry resulted in a further decline in what remained of the influence of Christian faith upon education in America. According to one statistic, there had been some six thousand academies in the United States in the 1850s. The Civil War and the sudden rise of the public high school that followed closed many of these private academies, where evangelical teaching had been at least possible if not always present. Now fear of an ensuing rampant apostasy, particularly among the young, caused a renewed interest in Christian education among some Christians. Foremost among these was the revivalist Dwight L. Moody, who founded two schools for training in Christian service, Northfield School for girls (1879) and Mount Hermon School for boys (1881).

At both Northfield and Mount Hermon, students were taught the Scriptures. Moody insisted upon a forthright presentation of the Bible as the truth of God. He regarded his schools as preparatory for Christian service, as his last public statement about the schools, in November 1899, shows:

> Five and twenty years ago in my native village of Northfield I planted two Christian schools for the training of boys and maidens in Christian living and consecration as teachers and missionaries of Jesus Christ. I bequeath as my legacy those training schools for Jesus to the churches of America, and I only ask that visitors to the beautiful native village where my ashes slumber on consecrated Round Top when they go there shall not be pained with the sight of melancholy ruins wrought by cruel neglect, but rather shall be greeted by the spectacle of two great, glorious lighthouses of the Lord, beaming out over the land, over the continent, over the world.

Moody's concern for the education of the poor was shared by a few others in the closing years of the nineteenth century. As cities swelled, some pastors saw clearly the need for the church to minister to the whole man, thereby giving rise to the "institutionalized church"—the church that is clinic, child-care center, club house, recreational center, library, and fellowship hall, as well as sanctuary. To these activities, Dr. Russell H. Conwell of Philadelphia added a night school, where students met in his Baptist Temple. The school, begun in 1884, consisted of working people and volunteer instructors. By 1888, the instruction had reached the collegiate level, and in time the Baptist Temple's night school became Temple University.

The churches of America were also becoming aware of their increasing responsibility to influence the education of the young, particularly since the majority of students were now enrolled in schools presenting a secular education exclusively. In 1903, the Religious Education Association was formed under the leadership of William Rainey Harper, then president of the University of Chicago. This society recognized that the Sunday School, which had developed some measure of strength throughout the nineteenth century, was simply not an adequate means of educating young people in the Christian faith. There must be support elsewhere. One amalgamation was the creating of "released-time" periods when public school students, at the request of their parents, could be dismissed from regular classes for classes in religious instruction. These classes were held on school premises in many districts, in church facilities in others. This practice continued until the Supreme Court's 1948 decision, *McCollum v. Champaign,* in which Mrs. Vashti McCollum complained that the Champaign, Illinois, schools discriminated against her son by providing religious instruction (she and her family were avowed atheists). In a significant and controversial decision the Court ended both the use of compulsory school time and public school facilities for the teaching of religious doctrine.

The twentieth century had begun with a deepening conflict between American education, both in theory and in practice, and Christian evangelicalism. In Chicago and later at Columbia University's Teachers College, Professor John Dewey, himself a former Sunday School teacher, was insisting that education should be a reproduction of life experience, a reconstruction of what the child innately knows. Given the opportunity to choose for himself, Dewey and his followers claimed, the child will make the decision that best satisfies his temperament and his own needs. Through the removal of objective standards and the instituting of relative measurements in their place, Dewey also did away with authority, except for the authority of personal experience. Dewey's thinking, of course, stood in direct opposition to Christian thought. He said, "I cannot understand how any realization of the democratic ideal as a vital moral and spiritual ideal in human affairs is possible without surrender of the conception of the basic division to which supernatural Christianity is committed."

The evangelical attitude was quite different. Orthodox Christianity still saw mankind as estranged from God because of sin. Man needed to be restored to a relationship with God through faith in the redemptive power of Jesus Christ. The Bible, as the inspired Word of God, made clear this revelation of God's abiding truth to man. Education might help to restore mankind but only if education began with the premise that man in fact needed to be restored.

The battle lines were being drawn on other fronts as well. Christianity was divided over social issues and the role of the church as an agency for social reform. Factions in the major denominations grew wider apart as colleges and seminaries took their stand on one side or another. The advocates of orthodoxy, Bible-centered and essentially other worldly, saw a dangerous influence in the German theology with its higher criticism of the Bible. Such scholarship, with its accompanying emphasis upon social action, was "modernistic." For themselves, the true believers held to "the fundamentals," the name given to a series of books published between 1910 and 1912, from which the term "fundamentalist" derives.

Such was the spirit within Christianity in the first decade of this century, when a group of ministers, drawn mostly from the New York City region and representing several major Protestant denominations, began contemplating a new Christian venture. It was to be a summer resort carefully designed for its architectual and horticultural beauty in a conducive natural setting. There people might refresh themselves in an atmosphere of recreation and spiritual restoration. As at Northfield, the conferences would present the world's most renowned Bible teachers. Perhaps some day there would also be a school.

2

Beginning the Stony Brook Experiment

The New York Times of July 14, 1907, announced

> the establishment of a summer assembly at Stony Brook, L.I., to do a
> work similar to that done at Chautauqua, Ocean Grove and elsewhere,
> possibly upon broader lines.

The organizers of this new corporation called themselves the
Stony Brook Assembly and had a twofold purpose, according to the
newspaper:

> First, the founding upon a permanent basis of an association to provide
> for an annual series of summer conferences at which present-day topics
> and problems in the religious, educational and civic world will be
> presented and discussed by masters of each department; and, second,
> the establishment of a colony of summer homes within easy reach of New
> York, where the surroundings will be pure and elevating.

The site chosen for this summer assembly and colony was the
historic village of Stony Brook, a quiet community in a cove off
Long Island Sound. As the tribal village of Wopowog, it had been
the home of the Setalcott Indians, a tribe associated with the
Montauks and their chieftain Wyandance. The Setalcotts sold their
land to a group of New England settlers on April 14, 1655.
Thereafter Wopowog became Stony Brook. The neighboring village
of Setauket, at first called Ashford, received its first English-
speaking residents at about the same time. By 1660 there was a
Presbyterian church in Setauket; by 1670 the sale of "strong drink
by retail" was permitted; by 1672 the sale of slaves was legalized.
The Stony Brook-Setauket area contributed an important spy
ring to the cause of the American Revolution, attested by General
George Washington's visit to the Roe Tavern, the spies'

headquarters in Setauket. The Battle of Setauket, fought on August 27, 1777, earned the Redcoats the everlasting hatred of local residents because the British stabled their horses in the Presbyterian church.

In the early nineteenth century, Stony Brook became a ship-building center. Captain Jonas Smith's company built schooners weighing as much as 400 tons, and there were other shipwrights as well: David T. Bayles, Daniel J. Williamson, and Captain Charles Hallock. Sailing packets and steamships made stops at Stony Brook harbor on their way to and from New York and ports farther east on Long Island. Cordwood cut from neighboring forests and hauled to Stony Brook's docks was shipped up and down the East coast.

At least two notable artists had come from Stony Brook during the nineteenth century. Micah Hawkins was the composer of the first successful American opera "The Saw-Mill" produced in 1824. More renowned is the genre painter William Sydney Mount, Micah Hawkins's nephew. Many of Mount's local scenes, such as "Dancing on the Barn Floor," "Long Island Farm-houses," and "Eel Spearing at Setauket," recreated the realism of rural American life for admirers of art everywhere.

But at the beginning of the twentieth century, Stony Brook had lost its industry and become just another somnolent village, a stop on the Long Island Rail Road's new sleek system. A few summer residents from New York knew of Stony Brook's placid pond and grist mill in service since 1699; they knew too its shady paths blooming with mountain laurel and rhododendron. Scarcely could its few hundred year-round residents expect, however, that their inconspicuous little village was about to become the hub of a Christian enterprise, a summer haven for thousands of God-fearing people of all ages and denominations, under the auspices of the Stony Brook Assembly.

*   *   *

The founder of the Stony Brook Assembly and the guiding spirit throughout the early period, was Dr. John F. Carson, pastor of the Central Presbyterian Church of Brooklyn, New York.

John Fleming Carson was the son of Scottish Covenanters from Northern Ireland who had emigrated to the United States in the mid-nineteenth century. As a young boy he had felt called of God to the ministry; he therefore prepared himself at the University of Pennsylvania and at Allegheny Theological Seminary, receiving his theological degree in 1885. Upon completion of his studies, John Carson was ordained and became the pastor of Central Presbyterian Church, where he remained for forty-two years, until his death on September 2, 1927.

During his lengthy ministry in Brooklyn, John Carson saw his congregation grow to become the second largest Presbyterian church in the United States. He was awarded two honorary degrees, both from Ursinus College, in 1893 and in 1911. That same year he was elected as Moderator of the General Assembly of the Presbyterian Church in the U.S.A. During World War I, he served as Chairman of the National Service Commission of the Presbyterian Church in the U.S.A.

Carson was a man of liberal spirit, free from parochialism. A tribute written shortly after his death by William Carter, pastor of the Throop Avenue Presbyterian Church in Brooklyn, described the man:

> There are some spirits that denominational lines cannot curb nor local environment hold within their bounds. John F. Carson was one of these. He was led outside the bounds of his own parish. He became a Christian Statesman, a man with a world vision, and with a deep and tender heart for the needs of all mankind.

Carson had known the Northfield conferences. He now hoped to interest his associates in a similar program nearer to New York City. In the winter of 1907, Stony Brook was suggested as a suitable location. Carson made a visit to the site proposed, a rising plot of ground opposite the Stony Brook depot of the Long Island Rail Road. At a glance he could see its many natural advantages. Here was a setting that combined the country meadow with proximity to the seashore; yet Stony Brook was not as crowded as were the beaches at Ocean Grove. Stony Brook had artesian wells from which to draw pure drinking water, large shade trees, and cool ravines. In short, Stony Brook was a summer idyll.

Carson began to consult with a number of friends. The Presbyterian evangelist J. Wilbur Chapman of Philadelphia approved both the idea and the location. Support likewise came from influential colleagues, pastors of prominent churches in Brooklyn. Together they formed their corporation, laid claim to the acreage in

Stony Brook, and prepared to open the Stony Brook Assembly in the summer of 1909.

The founders concurred on the necessity of establishing a common statement of their Christian belief that would also identify the purposes of the Stony Brook Assembly. The doctrinal statement they devised is broad, orthodox, yet free from denominationalism or labels. It remains as the Platform of Principles, a part of the charter granted to The Stony Brook School by the State of New York. It reads as follows:

Platform of Principles

  I. The divine inspiration, integrity, and authority of the Bible.
 II. The Deity of our Lord Jesus Christ.
III. The need and efficacy of the sacrifice of the Lord Jesus Christ for the redemption of the world.
 IV. The presence and power of the Holy Spirit in the work of redemption.
  V. The divine institution and mission of the Church.
 VI. The broad and binding obligation resting upon the Church for the evangelization of the world.
VII. The consummation of the Kingdom in the appearing of the glory of the great God and our Saviour Jesus Christ.

During that summer of 1909, the initial meetings of the Stony Brook Assembly were held in a large tent. Some who attended also lived in tents on the property, while others rented available cottages nearby or took rooms in the homes of Stony Brook villagers. But the plans of the Assembly called for greater luxury than this. According to its prospectus, the Assembly proposed to lay out some three hundred acres for building plots, conference grounds, and "a delightful waterside park."

An auditorium, shaped like the then-popular Billy Sunday tabernacles but much more permanent in structure, was ready for the second season of the Assembly in 1910.

"The Auditorium has been erected," wrote a reporter in *The Brooklyn Daily Eagle,*

and this magnificent building shows the high level upon which the association will carry out its improvements. There is nothing cheap or temporary about it. It is a surprise to all and impresses the visitor at once with the thought that here is an enterprise that is building for the future in a most substantial way. One can easily believe, in view of what has been done, that the association will complete its improvements in a substantial manner.

The four conferences held that summer were unusual for their time. The season began with a conference on current problems in society—child labor, housing, the cost of living. The second conference was "Farmers' Week." A third week concentrated upon the evangelization of young people, particularly young immigrants, through the work of the Young Men's and Young Women's Christian Associations. The fourth week was the season's highlight, a Bible conference with leading Bible teachers of the day participating. At summer's end, *The Brooklyn Daily Eagle* ran a half-page spread on the rapid development of the conferences.

By 1912, the Stony Brook Assembly commanded sufficient interest for *The Brooklyn Daily Eagle* to devote an entire page of each issue to news of the conference and abstracts of sermons by Dr. Carson and other speakers. Carson's close associates now were nearly all Presbyterian ministers, including William Hiram Foulkes, Ford C. Ottman, David G. Wylie, William L. McEwan, and Maitland Alexander. All of them were well-educated men, some with degrees from European seminaries as well as Princeton, Yale, or Union seminaries. Their accomplishments had earned them listing in *Who's Who in America*. They were respected leaders in their denomination.

These clergymen found that their lives intertwined around their mutual interests in service for God in their denomination and at the Stony Brook conferences. Their religion was orthodox but thoroughly enlightened; their preaching was evangelical without being emotional. They could scarcely be accused of other-worldliness. In fact, some of the stricter brethren considered them worldly because they enjoyed the good things of this life while looking to the life-to-come. Ottman, for example, is remembered as a distinguished dresser, a gentleman who enjoyed the finest corona cigars. He and some of the other leaders of the Stony Brook Assembly would seat themselves in some shady spot, lean back in their wicker chairs, and puff contentedly on their cigars. When a conference guest who disapproved of smoking launched into a reprimand, Ottman without so much as removing the offending cigar from his mouth would reach into his vest pocket and produce a railroad schedule to indicate the guest's options.

What held these several men together theologically was their affirmation of the Assembly's Platform of Principles. It was a platform, as Wylie said, "well built, wisely built, built in prayer, in faith in God, in Jesus Christ, in the Word of God, and in the gospel as a system of religious principles and doctrines which meets the requirements of mankind."

By the end of World War I, the conferences had grown so that, throughout a single season, several thousand people attended the evening meetings that were always open to the public; hundreds in the course of the summer were now living in neighboring cottages or in the newly constructed summer hotels.

Dr. Carson and his associates had been able to obtain donors who gave substantial gifts for the improvement of the conference grounds. In 1915, the large frame residence named Hopkins Hall was built through a gift from Ferdinand T. Hopkins of New York. This three-story building became the residence for conference guests who had been used to tenting or finding accommodations throughout the village.

Robert Johnston, a merchant from St. Louis, provided funds for a second residence, Johnston Hall, erected in 1918. The widow of J. Wilbur Chapman gave in his memory the funds with which to pave and landscape the main drive onto the conference property, known as Chapman Parkway.

Stony Brook's constituents were drawn primarily by the quality of preaching, but with the famous preachers also came the gospel musicians of the day. Chapman's associate, for example, was Charles M. Alexander, founder of the Pocket Testament League and composer of numerous hymns and gospel songs, including "That Will Be Glory for Me."

Thus, summer after summer the program of Bible teaching and music, matched with a delightful environment, brought more and more people to Stony Brook. But Carson had an even broader vision than could be achieved through annual summer conferences. Almost from the very first, he had thought about establishing a college preparatory school of the caliber of the Hill or Lawrenceville schools on the grounds of the Stony Brook Assembly. He had waited for the Assembly to gain stability and for a constituency of friends and supporters to become available. The intervention of World War I delayed him further; nor did he know the right man to lead such a school.

In the spring of 1921, Ford Ottman suggested to John Carson that they interview Frank E. Gaebelein, the twenty-two-year-old son of their friend, Dr. Arno C. Gaebelein. Ottman knew both father and son; Carson knew only Arno Gaebelein, but what he knew of the father recommended the son as a candidate.

Arno Gaebelein had emigrated from Germany to the United States in 1879, at the age of eighteen. He had been educated in the German *gymnasium,* but he was largely a self-taught man, a scholar of deep insight, a linguist, a prophetic expositor. He became an ordained minister in the German Methodist Episcopal Church, but his widest ministry was as editor of the magazine *Our Hope* and as a Bible teacher at various conferences. He was, in fact, one of the featured speakers at the Stony Brook Assembly's Prophetic Conference.

He had married Emma Fredericka Grimm, who bore three sons—Paul Whitefield, Arno Wesley, and Frank Ely—and a daughter, Claudia, who died in infancy. Frank Ely Gaebelein was born on March 31, 1899, in Mount Vernon, New York.

The Gaebelein home was far less strict than the stereotyped German family. There was, for example, no pressure regarding religious devotion from either parent upon the children. "Our home was a Christian home," Frank Gaebelein says, "not because my father was a noted preacher or because my mother was constantly talking to my brothers and me about religion, but because of the good sense with which they lived their faith. They never told me to read the Bible; yet I began to do so very early. I'm sure I learned to give some part of each day to the Scriptures from seeing my father and mother."

In much the same way, his father's example influenced Frank Gaebelein's development as a musician. Arno Gaebelein and his eldest son played four-hand arrangements of major piano works, while little Frank sat listening. The urge to imitate led him to the piano to pick out by ear a familiar song. Then, in order not to forget where to begin the next time, he cut a notch in the wood panel above the keys. Not unexpectedly, his father decided soon after to provide formal piano lessons.

From that time until 1920, Frank Gaebelein aspired to be a concert pianist. A second and not unrelated aspiration was to be a mountain climber. When he was just eleven years old, he was taken to Colorado with his family for a summer holiday. There he saw the Rocky Mountains, some of the peaks still snow-covered; he saw parties of mountaineers leaving for their climbs and heard some of them, upon their return, telling the thrill of standing upon the pinnacle of a mountain. From this experience he knew he wanted to climb.

Back home in New York State, he learned stamina from hard trudges in the Catskill Mountains. Later he came to know the Grand Tetons in Wyoming; not until 1938, however, did he taste his first Alpine climbing, on Mount Hood in Oregon. Eventually he fulfilled his boyhood wish with successful climbs up Mount Orizaba in Mexico (North America's third highest peak), some of the Chamonix Aiguilles, volcanoes in Iceland, and the Canadian Rockies he came to love so well.

Gaebelein also came to treasure his relationships with other mountaineers, including Professor I. A. Richards of Harvard, who read the Scripture lesson on one occasion when Gaebelein preached at the Sunday worship service of the Canadian Alpine Club. Another companion was the great French climber and guide Lionel Terray with whom he climbed in the French Alps.

In the fall of 1916, Gaebelein enrolled at the University College of New York University. On the Bronx campus he enjoyed a full college experience. His academic major was English, and he wrote for both the yearbook and the undergraduate newspaper. He was head of his fraternity chapter, Kappa Sigma, and lived in the fraternity house on Sedgewick Avenue, just off the University Heights campus.

There was also time for athletics. He ran on the varsity mile relay team coached by Emil von Elling. Von Elling, a fiery little man, instilled in each runner a sense of responsibility to the team. The fact that Frank Gaebelein earned his place on the relay squad is sufficient testimony of his ability, but it was not his strength as a runner that the aged Von Elling, one of the most respected track coaches in America, remembered many years later: It was Gaebelein's Christian influence upon his coach and teammates.

In addition to all these activities, Frank Gaebelein still gave time to music and was the piano soloist performing with the University Glee Club regularly, and he gave occasional recitals as well, holding fast to his early ambition to be a concert musician.

When the United States became involved in the Great War in Europe, Gaebelein enlisted in the officer training program, somewhat against the wishes of his parents and qualified for and received his commission as a second lieutenant of infantry in the United States Army. At the age of nineteen he was sent to Plattsburgh Barracks Training Camp, in upstate New York, where he trained recruits until the Armistice in November 1918. Then he returned to New York University in the middle of his junior year.

This interim in his life as a collegian had some part in a maturing decision. His months of military service had taken Frank Gaebelein away from the piano, and although he resumed both his piano study and performances, he no longer did so with the singleness of purpose that had marked his intentions previously.

"My interest in English studies and in writing was growing," he has said. Subsequently he would choose graduate studies in literature and composition rather than further music instruction at a conservatory. By the time he had graduated from New York University, the course of his life had shifted away from thoughts of a professional career in music. "As I look back," Gaebelein can say, "I see that all this was providential."

Frank Gaebelein, elected to Phi Beta Kappa and named a candidate for a Rhodes Scholarship, went to Harvard in the fall of 1920 for graduate study in English and comparative literature. His teachers included John Livingston Lowes and Irving Babbitt. But by far the most important teacher in Frank Gaebelein's experience at Harvard was Dean L. B. R. Briggs, whose many administrative and scholarly responsibilities did not prevent him from teaching a demanding course in writing. As a writer Gaebelein had been praised by previous teachers for the "ease and elegance" of his prose. Dean Briggs thought otherwise and reprimanded his graduate student for a style he thought too florid.

But if the style was flawed, Dean Briggs found much to commend in the thought of young Gaebelein. He was so impressed, in fact, by Gaebelein's work overall that he entered his pupil in the end-of-year competition for commencement addresses, as the representative speaker from the Graduate School. Much to Gaebelein's surprise, his speech, "In Behalf of Music," was chosen. Then followed seeming disaster: the commencement address must be memorized and declaimed.

Frank Gaebelein was no public speaker; he had had a speech hesitancy, almost a stuttering, that added embarrassment to his natural reluctance. It was arranged that Gaebelein should report to a teacher of rhetoric and speech for practice in delivering his remarks. Dr. Gaebelein recalls the experience: "After only a few minutes of my first lesson, the professor had judged me a hopeless case. I had no vocal projection, no sense of pacing. I was accenting all the wrong words. I was just awful."

Word of the impending humiliation must have reached Dean Briggs, and in a gesture of exemplary concern for his student, the busy man undertook personally to prepare Frank Gaebelein as a speaker. "He took me one night into Sanders Theatre where the commencement exercises were to be held, and told me to begin. I could barely see him moving from place to place throughout the auditorium, calling out instructions to me—'A little louder, please,'—and so on. He even appeared in the last row of the balcony with a word of helpful advice. We went through the speech several times, each time with my assurance growing. When the time came for me to speak, I was ready." It was the first major experience in public speaking for a man who would become recognized as a remarkably persuasive and effective speaker.

This was the man—tall, straight, already balding—whom John Carson and Ford Ottman arranged to meet at a New York restaurant, Billy the Oysterman's. According to Gaebelein, "We sat down to our meal, and they asked me a lot of questions about my plans—I had received a college teaching offer—and then began to ask about how I thought a school could be started, what needed to be done in the way of getting a faculty, what should be included in the curriculum, and so on."

Carson and Ottman excused themselves from the table and, removing themselves none too subtly to another table, left Frank Gaebelein to wonder what they were discussing. After a short interval, they rejoined their young guest and made their offer: Would he take over the organizing of the school? "I was thoroughly shocked," Dr. Gaebelein notes. "Remember, I was wholly without experience of the kind being required of me. And I was not a preparatory school graduate. In fact, before I visited the grounds of what was to become The Stony Brook School, I had never been on a preparatory school campus."

Yet John Carson was no mean judge of character. He had seen something in his first meeting with Frank Gaebelein that satisfied his expectations of what a schoolmaster should be. He was willing to trust God that this young man, with so fine a background of Christian family and personal faith, with so fine a record of academic and musical achievement—this man would perform his duties ably.

Gaebelein returned to Harvard from his interview with Carson and Ottman a troubled man. He had never seriously considered secondary school teaching; now he had been asked to head such a school. He did not doubt that he could learn to be a school administrator, but was this what he wanted to do with his life? The decision, arrived at after much prayer and consultation with one or two advisers, was to accept the offer of the Stony Brook Assembly. He set his own salary at $2400 per year.

In September 1921, Frank Gaebelein found himself principal (the term applied until changed to headmaster in the 1930s) of a school without faculty or students, without classrooms or books, without anything more than a name and a board of trustees to believe in the reality that one year later, through the providence of God, The Stony Brook School would open. Aristotle said, "What we have to learn to do, we learn by doing." Gaebelein took a small office in the Presbyterian Building at 156 Fifth Avenue in New York. One of his first acts was to draft a brochure describing the School as it was to be, calling it "an enterprise in Christian conservation," and announcing the School's motto, "Character before Career," a phrase coined by Ford Ottman. In the brochure he wrote:

> The aim of the school is to provide, in a Christian atmosphere and through Christian teachers, a sound education with a spiritual content, an education that has regard for the souls of our youth as well as for their bodies and their minds. To this end, the study of the English Bible and the fundamentals of Christianity will have a place of first importance in the curriculum.

The essential task facing Frank Gaebelein was that of creating a curriculum that would fulfill the desire of the founders and place the teaching of the Bible squarely at its center. In accepting the position as head of the new school, Gaebelein had also accepted a commission to do something that had not been done successfully in America in the twentieth century—to organize, staff, equip, and conduct a school in which the central focus would be upon the study of the Bible as the written revelation of God's truth, without any diminishing of intellectual standards, without any compromise of what Alfred North Whitehead called "the pursuit of excellence."

Of itself Bible study in the Stony Brook curriculum would not have made the School unique nor even unusual. Many schools have long offered courses in religion or sacred studies that include surveys of the Bible and the close reading of selected books of Scripture. But Stony Brook was not proposing to *include* the Bible; rather, the curriculum was to take its shape around the central fact that the Bible is the Word of God, God's truth. By the very nature of its existence, Stony Brook would consider the Bible as integral to its life and continuance.

Frank Gaebelein did not know how this would be done. In the months that followed, however, one thing became clear in his thinking: the study of the Bible must not be merely tangential to the rest of the curriculum. It must take its place in the formal course of study with all the dignity merited by the Bible's stature as a work of literature and as the primary document of the Christian faith. Now, fifty years later, the Bible retains its central position in the Stony Brook curriculum, although the methods of teaching have changed somewhat over the years.

At one time the Bible, like much of other literature, was taught in a wholly didactic manner, the instructor lecturing while students dutifully recorded his comments. Bible was also taught as a wholly separate subject unrelated to other courses. For both of these reasons the Bible courses at Stony Brook were not always as successfully conducted as their inherent merit required. An insensitive seminarian dictating his graduate notes on systematic theology to a class of ninth-grade boys suggests one extreme of the problem.

After World War II, a distinct trend in teaching, particularly the teaching of literary texts, reached the schools from various universities and graduate schools. Under the catch-all title of "the new criticism," this formalistic approach to any piece of literature—as a written work the Bible is literature in this sense—began with the premise that the literary work is an entity of its own, that it has its own independent significance apart from the biography of its author or the history of his era, and that the literature under study ought to be examined for what it says of itself. In the specific field of Bible teaching this method became known as "inductive Bible study," as then taught at The Biblical Seminary in New York (now New York Theological Seminary). Three young teachers of Bible came to Stony Brook from this seminary, bringing with them the freshness of this approach to the study of the Scriptures. Among them was Karl E. Soderstrom, now chairman of the Bible Department. In his early enthusiasm, Soderstrom tended to overreact to the typical Stony Brook student's approach to a problem in Bible reading. "I went in to the library one day in my first year," says Soderstrom, "and here were all these guys sitting around the tables with huge, dusty Bible commentaries, taking in every word. They had almost no idea of what the Bible itself said, but they knew what Matthew Henry or Charles Spurgeon said. I told them to close those commentaries for good!"

Not only did Soderstrom lead Bible teaching toward a closer study of the text itself, but he also merged his classes at the eleventh and twelfth grades with the English classes. He does not feel that the merger diminished either the importance or the effect of Bible study at Stony Brook. "On the contrary, it gives us an easier *entre* into other areas of our students' thinking and behavior. We used to suffer from this 'Bible class syndrome,' with students adopting a whole new set of attitudes and postures just because we're now in *Bible* class. It was somehow quite remote from the rest of their day. Now we're talking about Job and Oedipus and Willy Loman, or the arguments in *Romans* and *Ecclesiastes* and in Camus or Dostoevsky or Kafka, all in the same setting. I think it's much more productive of serious thought about the claims the Bible makes than our previous system."

Stony Brook still conducts separate courses in Bible in grades seven through ten, since it is felt that a solid grounding and familiarity with the Bible is necessary before the more mature correlated studies with other literature can be undertaken in the final two years. "The Bible, quite apart from the fact that it is God's revelation of eternal truth to mankind," says Dr. Gaebelein, "is still the most complete record we have of the origins of our Western culture, the so-called Judeo-Christian tradition. Anyone who gives himself to a thoroughgoing study of the Bible has enjoyed an intellectual experience more than comparable to an introduction to Plato's *Dialogues*."

Convinced of the validity of his view, the young Frank Gaebelein began to consult with experienced schoolmasters. Among those whom he visited was Mather A. Abbott, then headmaster of the renowned Lawrenceville School. "One of my ineffaceable memories," says Dr. Gaebelein, "is that of knowing Mather Abbott. I can see him now as he told me, 'Every headmaster should feel that his boys are sent him from God." Dr. Abbott, in an interview in *The Christian Science Monitor,* later recalled his meeting with Gaebelein:

> He came with his youthful enthusiasm, telling me that he was going to make the Bible the major study and teach it three times a week, and I was tremendously impressed. I said to myself as he sat there, "Would that I were he! Is it possible? Can he do it?" Well, he seems to have done it. I would that I could teach the Bible that often in my school, but I cannot have it more than once a week. I do not believe there is another school in the country that is doing it. It takes courage to put spiritual things first nowadays.

Stony Brook's boys were to do more than merely study the Bible: they were to memorize large numbers of passages. It became a familiar sight on the campus to see a senior, perhaps, with a packet of index cards in his hands, his lips moving silently, a swift check of a forgotten word on the card, the shuffling of a completed passage to the bottom of the pile. Frank Gaebelein became a terrorizer of any occasionally indolent student who dared to be sloppy about his memory work. Spotting him somewhere on the campus, the headmaster would stride over to him and accost him with a reference. Not to be able to recite on demand was placing oneself in grave danger of the headmaster's displeasure.

Many stories are told about the experiences of alumni who remembered a memorized verse of Scripture at an opportune moment. One of the most dramatic occurred when John S. Medd, Jr., '40, was about to enter the Battle of Coral Sea, in May 1942. The commander of his submarine had gathered his men around for a brief devotional service. He was reading Psalm 91. Suddenly the lights went out, and the reading stopped. But from the crowd a voice picked up the text—"He shall give his angels charge over thee to keep thee in all thy ways," and so on to the end of the psalm. When the lights were restored, the commander asked the speaker to identify himself and to tell how he happened to know the psalm. "I had to memorize it, sir," said John Medd. "At Stony Brook you have to memorize Bible verses in order to graduate."

Not all Gaebelein's advisers were so ready to congratulate him on the plans for the proposed school. Some were certain that in time, like the many other schools whose founders had intended a religious emphasis, Stony Brook would succumb to whatever pressures cause such a school to abandon its principles. In some instances, this discontinuity of purpose results from changes in administration; in other instances, from changes that reflect a school's adherence to popular trends; in still other instances, from a struggle for control between supporters of the founding charter and those who would alter it. In almost every such situation, no matter what its apparent cause, the real cause for the failure of a school to hold firmly to a single, consistent role has much to do with money.

As taxpayers everywhere know, education is costly. Private education, because it depends almost wholly upon its own resourcefulness to maintain itself, is gravely underfinanced. Schools and colleges are examining every means possible to cut expenses without endangering quality. Some institutions are merging; others have created co-operative plans or consortia; some have closed in a state of bankruptcy.

Any school based on principles must expect to face the test of its commitment to those principles in the crucible of experience. So much more so the Christian school, for by the very nature of its commitment it shuts itself off from most sources of financial backing. The Apostle Paul observed that "not many mighty, not many noble" are called; few among the wealthy are supporters of the Christian school. Providentially there are some, and Stony Brook has been unusually fortunate in obtaining gifts from a few foundations and individual philanthropists.

The Clark Foundation, for example, sustains the cost of tuition each year for a sizable number of minority students of underprivileged status. Another, the Staley Foundation, endows an annual lectureship. Among individual donors is DeWitt Wallace, co-editor and publisher of *The Reader's Digest*. Introduced to Stony Brook by Dr. Billy Graham a few years ago, Mr. Wallace has contributed generously to endow a number of scholarships. The family of the late Robert S. Swanson has also contributed frequently to the School, their latest gift being a one-million dollar gymnasium.

But such gifts as these are rare. By far the bulk of a Christian school's financial assistance comes from a continuing stream of gifts in the $25-to-$100 range, expressions of support from a nucleus of faithful constituents; at least, so it is at Stony Brook.

Those who doubted that the Stony Brook intentions could be fulfilled anticipated that the prospective clientele would lose interest; that an insufficient number of qualified teachers could be found; that boys would not really be happy in a spiritual environment; and that, with all these setbacks, financial difficulties would result from which The Stony Brook School could not avoid slipping into compromise. From compromise, the next step would be to an indistinguishable conformity with the mass of boys' college preparatory schools. To these critics it seemed only a matter of time before Stony Brook's inevitable financial needs would bring about a readjustment to the realities of independent education.

Perhaps because these critics were themselves too much a part of the conventional system of education, they could not observe that some parents and others interested in American education were looking for an alternative to the educational philosophies that prevailed. These parents were looking, in short, for the kind of education a school such as Stony Brook might offer. Looking back over the School's first seven years, a magazine writer for *Long Island Life* gave this explanation:

> Many parents still believe, with good reason, that character is possible, that it is within the latent capacity of boys to learn to order their lives on principle. When such parents can find an educational institution in which the development of that capacity is encouraged they choose for their boys such an atmosphere, in preference to one that discourages spiritual growth. This explains the extraordinary success of Stony Brook School. Educational tendencies being as they are, a school that gives the English Bible a place in its curriculum as prominent as that of any other subject, and that has developed a uniquely appealing Christian atmosphere, is as sure to grow as a potato in Suffolk County.

The first catalogue announced how the School intended to create and maintain its Christian quality. It was not to be a religious school nor a school with a pietistic emphasis; it would be a distinctly

Christian school. Its faculty must be thoroughly committed to the Christian faith and to its exemplification in their lives.

With these facts in view, the teachers for The Stony Brook School have been selected. No man will be employed whose religion is a mere profession. No matter what his antecedents, he will not have a place on the faculty unless his Christianity is vital, unless he burns with the desire to lead others to the faith that creates true character. For upon the teacher rests the problem of making Christianity real to the boy.

So Frank Gaebelein set about to obtain Christian teachers for his new school. "It has long been a source of amazement to me that the first teachers engaged were both men of wide experience," he says. "Yet something about the plans we had for Stony Brook touched them and made them respond to the opportunity." Arthur DeLancey Ayrault and William Oncken were those first two masters hired. Ayrault, a Phi Beta Kappa graduate of Columbia University, had been a headmaster and teacher of mathematics for over thirty years. Oncken, who had been teaching at Riverdale School, was trained at the University of Bern in Switzerland. His wife, born Baroness Eve von Korning, was a concert pianist, a graduate of the National Conservatory in Helsinki, Finland; she became the third faculty member to be hired. "That people of this caliber consented to work under a mere beginner who had never had any administrative experience in education at all!" "To my mind," says Gaebelein, "this is characteristic of the gracious spirit of self-abnegation that has done so much for Stony Brook throughout its history."

From his nucleus of three instructors, Frank Gaebelein proceeded to hire a full faculty of nine, plus a registered nurse and a secretary. He was himself a teacher of English. The pastor of the Old First Presbyterian Church in Huntington, Long Island, the Reverend Edward J. Humeston, taught the courses in Bible. An outstanding college athlete named Clyde Mellinger, from Penn State, came to teach science courses and to conduct the athletic program.

The faculty was gradually assembled, but where were the students? "In this first year," Gaebelein confesses, "we had an exalted idea of the large number of students that we could secure, but time passed and they did not come. Even in mid-summer there was practically no enrollment. The thrill when the first enrollments were received is still fresh in my memory—Tom and Marius Brohard of El Paso, Texas. I have always admired the faith of their parents at such a distance in entrusting their boys to a new school."

At about the same time, John Barton from Tenafly, New Jersey was enrolled, and this was further encouragement for the young schoolmaster that his school would in fact have a student body. But Frank Gaebelein was no desk-bound optimist. Even close to opening day he was making personal calls to the homes of inquirers, looking for any possible prospects. By September 13, 1922, he had enrolled twenty-seven boys.

The inaugural ceremonies of The Stony Brook School brought a distinguished group of academicians to the campus of the fledgling school. "The program was an impressive one," Dr. Gaebelein recalls. "It's doubtful whether it has ever been surpassed at Stony Brook." Brief statements of greeting were brought on behalf of American schools, universities, and churches. Then the headmaster gave his first address, called "The Plan and Scope of The Stony Brook School." In part, Frank Gaebelein said,

> Education without character is a dangerous thing. For character, not intellectual agility, is the source of right living. But character itself has a source. It springs not from moral maxims, rules of conduct, proverbs, or thou-shalt-nots. Its derivation is higher. It grows out of religious experience—the effective religious experience that is the result of the gospel of our Lord and Saviour Jesus Christ.

To create an environment in which Christian character might be nurtured, Gaebelein listed "five principles for the Christian school," analogous to and consistent with the Platform of Principles of the Stony Brook Assembly.

1. The Christian school must be comparatively small with a correspondingly large staff of teachers.
2. The teachers in the Christian school must qualify as masters of their subjects.
3. The Christian school must maintain an atmosphere that is consistent with its aim.
4. Spiritual things must have their rightful place in the Christian school—and that place is the first place.
5. The Christian school must ever preserve a nice balance between the religious, scholastic, and recreative phases of its work.

A few words to expand on each of these points, and then the address concluded with a call for a renewed Christian humanism, similar to that found at Vittorino's school in Mantua five centuries before:

> A humanism that would have every essential study taught in the most efficient way possible, that would never yield one jot in the field of scholarship; a humanism that, in its broad application, would help each individual student to solve his own unique intellectual and spiritual problems—this will guide the faculty of The Stony Brook School in their glorious adventure in Christian education—an adventure that will serve the Church of Jesus Christ by conserving the faith of her youth, an adventure that will serve the nation by giving to it, year by year, a body of young men of stalwart character, well-taught and nurtured in the faith.

It was, as these few excerpts demonstrate, a stirring speech, a challenge to the whole enterprise of Christian education, the more remarkable because it had been delivered by a novice. Yet it was more than theory, for the speech delineated the manner in which Frank Gaebelein had already begun to confront the major problems in Christian education—the problems of "correlation" or, as he would later say, "integration into the all-embracing truth of God."

The main speaker for the occasion was President Francis L. Patton, former president of Princeton University and of Princeton Theological Seminary. In his remarks, this distinguished educator created an expression, "the Fourth R"—religion, to join reading, 'riting, and 'rithmetic as the core of education. It was a phrase widely repeated, and as the School grew and its reputation spread, journalists took "the Fourth R" as a catchword to describe Stony Brook. In *The Christian Science Monitor*'s feature story about the School, the education editor wrote,

> The visitor also observes that although religion is a fourth R at Stony Brook, and Bible study is a major subject, the boys are as fun-loving and active as normal schoolboys are everywhere. The development of the spiritual side is as natural as breathing and is accepted as a part of true education.

And Dorothy Gow, the education columnist for the *New York Evening Post*, wrote,

> You've probably heard of Stony Brook, L. I., as a favorite summer resort in connection with the many conferences in religious education that are held there each summer, but I wonder how many Long Islanders ap-

preciate what a strong, fine school for boys has developed in their midst during the last ten years . . . a school now known all over this country and in many foreign ones. A live school, growing, progressive, modern . . . an actively Christian school that has added a fourth "R" to the three fundamental "R's" of learning (religion as well as reading, 'riting and 'rithmetic). Not a religion of creed but rather of spiritual experience . . . a character building that comes from within rather than from rules.

* * *

The inaugural ceremonies at an end and the many hundreds of guests departed, the task of schoolmastering had just begun for Frank Gaebelein and his faculty. The time had come to fulfill the pledges made in conversation, in writing, and in public address. For the first time the headmaster of The Stony Brook School felt the weight of his responsibilities—a weight he would carry for forty-one years.

The entire school operation was housed in Hopkins Hall, the only building on the premises equipped with a heating system. Within a few weeks after classes began, eleven additional boys enrolled bringing the student body to thirty-eight. Seven of these were day students commuting from the vicinity. Hopkins Hall, therefore, was the residence for thirty-one boys and all but one of the faculty and their families. In spite of these crowded conditions, the headmaster was able to report to the board of trustees, "There has been no friction among the teachers—or the wives of the teachers."

The inaugural student body was diverse in age, ability, and background. The youngest was eight years old; two boys were nineteen. They came from eight states (New York, New Jersey, Pennsylvania, Massachusetts, Maryland, Ohio, Oklahoma, and Texas); two boys were from China. Some of these boys were excellent scholars; others had experienced severe academic difficulty in their previous schools. But the consensus of the faculty, after only five weeks of instruction, showed that most boys seemed to be responding favorably to the small classes and virtually individualized instruction they were receiving.

There were, of course, many problems. Clyde Mellinger was unable to perform laboratory experiments in his chemistry class because he had no place to set up his laboratory equipment. "I shudder now to think how we solved that problem," says Dr.

Gaebelein—and, indeed, he does shudder! "We fixed up a room in the basement, next to the boiler room."

Not all the students were happy at the new school. One month after its beginning, Frank Gaebelein faced his first instance of major discipline. His decision was that the offending student, whose violations included the use of "profane and indecent language," had had a detrimental influence upon the rest of the School, particularly because he was an older boy, and should be separated from the School.

In general, however, morale was high. A significant contributor to the good spirit was the athletic program under Mellinger's leadership. In spite of the handicap of having so few boys and even fewer with adequate size and playing experience, Stony Brook fielded a football team in its first autumn. Quite expectedly, the team was defeated in its games against Hempstead and Patchogue high schools, but a tradition of competition and support for athletics throughout the School had been firmly grounded.

Frank Gaebelein sensed the spirit of the School and wrote in his first report to the board, on October 18, 1922:

> It is the unanimous opinion of the faculty that the great principle upon which the school has been founded has already been proved true.

Athletics, of course, was not the only diversion offered the boys at Stony Brook. The Carson Literary Society had been formed and was already at work on its first publication, a journal called *The Adventurer*. A radio club and a chess club were also organized. Madame Oncken had started an instrumental ensemble, and Frank Gaebelein would often entertain the School by playing piano selections on the grand piano in the lobby of Hopkins Hall.

By December of that first year, Frank Gaebelein had decided that two significant adjustments in present policy were necessary. The original plan for Sunday worship had been that the entire School family should attend the Setauket Presbyterian Church. This was still a satisfactory arrangement, but he now favored a schedule of services, at least once a month, on the campus. Eventually, weekly Sunday worship service was established so that over the years the preachers who have spoken at Stony Brook include some of the most renowned ministers, teachers, missionaries, and professors, as well as evangelists.

The second change recommended called for a resident Bible teacher able to teach a full schedule and to counsel students. Frank Gaebelein turned from teaching English to teaching Bible, a decision that Stony Brook's succeeding classes over four decades felt in no small measure! From the preparation for his new teaching assignment came the germ for his first book about the Bible, *Exploring the Bible.*

Gilbert P. Inglis was the first graduate of The Stony Brook School, receiving his diploma in 1923. The son of Dr. Robert Scott Inglis, a Presbyterian pastor in Newark, New Jersey, Inglis gave Stony Brook's program of college preparation and admission a notable beginning when he was accepted at Princeton.

The school had weathered its first year. The founders and supporters of Stony Brook were given additional cause to be gratified by the news that the Regents of the University of the State of New York would approve the school after only its first year's work. This was a most unusual tribute from a discriminating academic board. It was the crowning delight for John Carson, whose faith and perseverance had brought the school into being.

The life of a bachelor schoolmaster was full of duty and responsibility. It might also have been lonely, had not Frank Gaebelein met Miss Dorothy Laura Medd of nearby Old Field, New York. He began courting her, riding back and forth from the campus to her home on an old horse Nancy, and later on a mustang Lum. They were married on December 8, 1923.

In courtship, the decision of a boarding school headmaster is not far different from that of a prince, for on his choice depends the good of the whole. Dorothy Medd Gaebelein, a graduate of Vassar College, was the perfect complement to her husband in his demanding position. Well-bred and intelligent, gracious yet determined, she set an example through forty years as the headmaster's wife for the wives of the faculty. Recognizing the intensity with which the pressures of boarding school life crowded in upon her husband, she learned how to provide that essential balance between hospitality and refuge, which only the privacy of a home can afford. Yet Mrs. Gaebelein remained in the background. A young teacher or student, whose knock at the Gaebelein's door was answered by the headmaster's wife, was never made to feel that he was intruding. Nor were there any doubts about the anonymity of boys in trouble or the confidence in which domestic problems within the faculty were treated. Whatever concerns Dr. Gaebelein may have shared with his wife remained discreetly confidential. "I pray in the abstract," she has said, "and I'm just as sure that God knows who I'm praying for."

Dorothy Gaebelein brought to Stony Brook her love for Long Island and its natural beauty. With her sister, Miss Miriam Medd, and with help from other friends in the community, such as Mr. and Mrs. John Mackie, she took the responsibility for transforming the somewhat scrubby conference grounds into a campus of varied and parklike design, making the Stony Brook campus a natural beauty spot at all seasons.

To Mrs. Gaebelein also fell the ticklish responsibility of acquainting faculty wives with some of their peculiar obligations as ladies on a boys' school campus. Privately she warned newcomers about the need for modesty in dress and recommended that on washday lingerie be placed on the lines as inconspicuously as possible. Unlike many boarding schools, Stony Brook has always welcomed the faculty wives and children to all meals; but Mrs. Gaebelein insisted that toddlers not be fed their mixed fruits and chopped liver from a baby jar during the meal. "It's not an appetizing sight for the boys," she told the young mothers.

Her hospitality was also well known among generations of students, many of whom visited the Gaebelein home weekly for a Tuesday evening prayer fellowship or for an informal Sunday evening of music and also Dr. Gaebelein's reading of a humorous essay or mystery story. Mrs. Gaebelein would scarcely be seen at these gatherings in her home, so cautious was she about intruding into relationships she considered to be essentially between men and boys.

Dorothy Gaebelein's greatest contribution to her husband's work, outside her responsibilities in the home, was to create in faculty wives a loyalty to Stony Brook matched only by that of their husbands.

*   *   *

Among the great numbers of persons who know and support The Stony Brook School, all know the name Gaebelein. It is common to find friends of the School who suppose that it was founded by Dr.

Arno C. Gaebelein, if not by his son. But Frank Gaebelein is quick to inform them, and to remind others, that Stony Brook was the vision of John Fleming Carson, that it was he who carried the principal burden for the founding of the Stony Brook Assembly and for the subsequent development of its school until his death on September 3, 1927. "Never forget," Dr. Gaebelein says today, "that Stony Brook is, in the providence of God, what she is today only because men like John Carson persevered to make it so."

Twenty years had passed since John Carson first invited his associates to band together and form the Stony Brook Assembly. In those years, a dreadful war had wracked the world; its aftermath of uncertainty and instability could still be felt. Yet out of that union of denominational leaders had come a strong Christian witness in the form of summer conferences; out of that fellowship of churchmen, inspired by the devotion and serene faith of Dr. Carson, had come a school dedicated to the training of youth who would place Christian character before career.

3

The Noblest of Occupations

In 1922 Frank Gaebelein was young and, except for his useful but brief experience as an infantry officer, without previous administrative responsibility. Yet he had two great assets essential to the task at Stony Brook: a rich store of faith and that irreducible quality in a schoolmaster, the mind of a scholar.

Frank Gaebelein's prior inexperience, however, was an asset in this peculiar case. Stony Brook represented a departure from the usual American secondary education, in both public and private schools. Current educational theory seemed tied to the teachings of John Dewey or his disciples, J. B. Watson, William Heard Kilpatrick, and Boyd H. Bode. Dewey advocated "social unification" with the child and the school as the focus around which society would center. In Dewey's view the aim of education was to enable the child freely to perceive "the inherited resources of the race, and to use his own powers for social ends." The result, of course, was the elimination of absolute standards of conduct or morality; instead, each child determined for himself the behavior most pleasing to him. This was Dewey's progressive education, a development of misconceived "democracy," as revealed in Bode's Book, *Democracy as a Way of Life:*

> Conduct on the part of communities or individuals must be evaluated with reference to its effect on promoting common interests among men. Liberty grows as the area of common interests is widened. Democracy then becomes identified with this principle of relativity, as contrasted with the absolutism of dictatorships. There is no middle ground.

Another interpreter of Deweyism, John L. Childs, dismissed objective standards in these words:

Since experience is an ongoing process, this view also means that finality
and absolute certainty are impossible. Absolute dogma must give place
to hypotheses.

Truths are the opinions, the beliefs, the hypotheses which have been
verified by experience. Since experience is ongoing in nature and conditions do change, absolute finality is not to be had.

The ultimate source, authority, and criterion for all belief and conduct
are to be found in ordinary human experience.

Hand in hand with this relativism went J. B. Watson's
behaviorism. "The behaviorist," he wrote, "recognizes no dividing
line between man and brute." Elsewhere Watson contended that
"the behaviorist finds no mind in his laboratory, sees it nowhere in
his subjects."

Stony Brook represented a return to what had been the first
tradition of American education—training young men in Christian
principles for Christian service. As such, the new school did not
require a headmaster who had been trained in the new behaviorism;
instead, Stony Brook required a man who would be free to develop a
curriculum based upon a surer foundation. With no other
pedagogical loyalties than his knowledge that "the fear of the Lord
is the beginning of wisdom," Frank Gaebelein was free to mold the
school as his faith and scholarship persuaded him was right. With
Thomas Arnold of Rugby, he determined that "what we must look
for here is, first, religious and moral principles; secondly, gen-
tlemanly conduct; thirdly, intellectual ability."

These qualities combined in the man to make him a Christian
educator without peer in this century. He is a writer, biblical
scholar, theologian, and preacher. Donald Barr, headmaster of the
Dalton School, has written in *Who Pushed Humpty Dumpty?*:

> In America, until recently, few educational innovators have actually run
> schools for very long. . . . The American style of innovation is
> *movemental*, manifesto-writing, association-founding, superior to the
> chores of authority, and frequently ignorant about children and
> teachers.

Frank Gaebelein was an exception to this rule. For forty-one years
he continued his leadership of The Stony Brook School. In that time
he also wrote more than a dozen books, including an improbable

novel about chess called *The Hollow Queen.* His other books were Bible studies or devotionals, such as *Four Minor Prophets, The Practical Epistle of James,* and *Looking Unto Him,* or volumes on the philosophy of Christian education, *Christian Education in a Democracy* and *The Pattern of God's Truth.*

Christian Education in a Democracy (1951) remains the definitive statement from the evangelical position. The book takes the position that the world is unregenerate in its estrangement from God, that neither the philosopher nor the psychologist can improve man's condition nor can man pull himself up by his ethical boot-straps. Education, if left in the hands of men in the same condition as those they would presume to educate, can hardly result in moral improvement. The solution is found in a return to education that centers itself about the unifying principle of God's truth revealed through the Living Word, Jesus Christ, and the written Word, the Holy Scriptures. The preface declares the author's point of view:

> There is nothing narrow about this answer to the search for the unifying principle of education. Jesus Christ is not a sectarian Person; bigger than any human attempt to define His significance, He is Himself the answer. Education is not theory, it is life; and the truest solution of its problem lies not in abstract principles but in a living Person.

In addition to being a successful writer himself, Frank Gaebelein was also generous with his time and gave helpful criticism to younger writers, especially those among his teachers who wished to write.

In my own case, Dr. Gaebelein has been both an inspiring and a demanding mentor. When I first attempted magazine writing, I sent him a copy of a manuscript draft, along with a letter expressing my dissatisfaction with the work. He replied with typical candor from his vacation site in Colorado:

> Thank you for your letter and for letting me see the enclosed article. I emphatically agree with your own dissatisfaction with it. To put it bluntly, this treatment of a serious and difficult subject, while bright and catchy, is superficial. As you yourself say, you have not yet resolved the problem in your own mind. One of the deficiencies of our Christian journalism is, I think, its tendency to brief, clever, and inadequate treatment of difficult and profound subjects.

I should strongly advise you to hold this article for further thought and rewriting, including expansion. It could grow into a four or five thousand word treatment such as a magazine might use in several installments. The subject is vitally important and *needs* discussion. I've thought about it and would like to take an hour to discuss it with you on my return. Please understand me. What you have done is not bad; it's just that it doesn't do the subject justice, as I believe you might do it justice with a great deal more consideration. Let's talk about it on my return in August.

We did talk it over, the article was thoroughly revised and improved and published. Thereafter, I frequently consulted Dr. Gaebelein and received his help, even after he had left Stony Brook and was busy with full-time writing and editing. I have known many fine teachers of composition but only one other whose critical sense has been as clear and unfailing as Frank Gaebelein's.

Nor did he restrict himself to his own faculty. In the 1930s, a young Long Island newspaperman feeling constrained of God to seek Christian training came to Gaebelein for advice. His name was Carl F. H. Henry, and he has since become a leading evangelical scholar, writer, and lecturer. When Dr. Gaebelein retired from Stony Brook in 1963, he joined Henry as co-editor of *Christianity Today*, the evangelical theological journal.

In 1941, Dr. Gaebelein was examined by a committee of bishops and presbyters of the Reformed Episcopal Church and ordained a deacon in that denomination; the following year, he was ordained a presbyter. Dr. Gaebelein preached in the chapels of the U.S. Military Academy, Union College, Lafayette College, Pennsylvania State University, St. Paul's Chapel at Columbia University, and other colleges and independent schools, such as Lawrenceville and Hotchkiss. For his work as a biblical scholar, theologian, and preacher he was made a honorary Doctor of Letters by Wheaton College in 1931. He was also awarded the degree of Doctor of Divinity by the Reformed Episcopal Seminary in 1951 and Doctor of Laws by Houghton College in 1960.

With all these activities crowding in upon him, Frank Gaebelein always reserved time for his favorite recreation, the serious playing of the piano. He will say now that he was only very ordinary, but just how well Dr. Gaebelein can play may be realized from the fact that he performed twice on the National Broadcasting Company's network program, "Music Is My Hobby." The well-known announcer and music commentator Milton Cross introduced the headmaster and described his playing as "like a professional." The program's producer called it "a stunning performance." He also played in recital over WQXR, the finest music station in New York City.

From time to time, Dr. Gaebelein would play at Stony Brook or perform in concert with a local symphony orchestra. His preference has always been decidedly classical, but he appreciates the originality and improvisation of newer forms of music. He has said, "We should be no more surprised to hear today's music on an electronic computer than Bach would be to hear his music, written for the clavichord, played upon a concert grand piano."

In one instance he had a mixed reaction to popular music. A community concert series had arranged to use Stony Brook's Carson Auditorium for several performances, including an appearance by the eminent jazz pianist Teddy Wilson and his quartet. Dr. Gaebelein entertained Wilson in his home and enjoyed their discussion on the relation between jazz and the classics. Later during the concert, a performer sang some torch songs, much to the sustained pleasure of the Stony Brook boys. After quite literally weaving her way through a rendition of "Squeeze Me," she switched to Gordon Jenkins' "New York's My Home." She sang the song as written, extolling the virtues of New York over other cities, and then a member of the quartet called out, "What about Stony Brook?" The vocalist crooned into her microphone,

> *Well, Stony Brook's a real fine town,*
> *It's got the greatest school*
> *And a headmaster that's real cool!*

That was too much for the headmaster, and he left the auditorium in chagrin.

The scope and quality of his productivity over the years made Gaebelein a man held in awe by many of his students and faculty. He was so nearly the fulfillment of popular notions of the Renaissance Man—scholar, writer, musician, athlete—that his students were sometimes surprised to discover that he was also full of a vibrant humor and enjoyed either telling a good joke or reading aloud from a favorite comic author. Some would have been amazed to know that Frank Gaebelein had once played the part of the simpleton knight Sir Andrew Aguecheek in a high school production of Shakespeare's *Twelfth Night.*

He was always athletic, challenging boys to contests of punting the football or slamming out a baseball. Once he found himself at the start of an impromptu race up Chapman Parkway—enough of a test that Stony Brook's track coach, Marvin Goldberg, sometimes uses it for early-season conditioning. Dr. Gaebelein drew upon his college relay experience but, as he says, he paid a heavy price for his comraderie. "I wobbled and staggered around in front of Carson Auditorium at the top of the hill until someone finally sent for the nurse. That was the end of my races against the boys."

Most students saw him, especially in his maturer years, as a towering intelligence ready with the irrefutable argument. To a senior student's demanding question, the reply might be, "I once wrote a book on that subject. It's in the library. Read it over the weekend, and we'll talk about it."

Charles Lamb said, "We are not quite at our ease in the presence of a schoolmaster because we are conscious that he is not quite at his ease in ours." Gaebelein was always a very busy man, often preoccupied with the multitude of concerns only a larger spirit can absorb. But one unwavering rule regarding his time always obtained. Both Mrs. Gaebelein and his secretaries had clear instructions to interrupt his work at any time when a boy came to his door. "I made it a practice," he says, "to step out of my office or study and say a few words to the boy. I could usually tell by his expression just how seriously he needed to see me right then."

Gaebelein's principal devotion was to these boys and to the School; most of his energy, both on and off the campus, was spent for the good of the School. But he was also active in the business of other organizations, serving as president of the American Tract Society, as both a trustee and a regent of the Dallas Theological Seminary, as vice-chairman of the Revision Committee for the Scofield Reference Bible, and as chairman of the Council for Religion in Independent Schools.

These duties took him away from the campus frequently; in the opinion of some faculty, too frequently. Once a young teacher, whose business with the absent headmaster seemed particularly pressing, suggested to Mrs. Gaebelein that it might be appropriate to fly a pennant from the flagpole when the headmaster was in residence. The young man, who might have been summarily informed of his impertinence, received instead an explanation of the importance of the headmaster's work. The fact was that Dr. Gaebelein used his many associations with off-campus organizations, and the personal relationships thereby established, to create an interest and enlarge the support for the School. In this respect, the School needed his absence as much as his presence.

Yet no matter whether or not the headmaster was on the campus, the fact of his intercessory prayer on behalf of the School, its faculty, and many of its students, daily and by name, was a known positive force. "It is literally true," says a trustee who has known the School since its Depression days, "that the effectual fervent prayers of Frank Gaebelein pulled the School through those years. It's as though he had taken hold of God and wrestled in prayer until he obtained the promise of blessing." The spiritual tone of the School, the attitude of a specific man or boy, the request of an alumnus facing temptation in college or military service, the sickness of a friend—these were equal causes for prayer.

Such a man could not help earning both the respect of his colleagues and the admiration of those who knew his compassionate spirit. He sought scholastic excellence, demanding it of himself and of others; he also possessed a genuine concern for people, although his businesslike and often brusque manner prevented a full appreciation of this trait by someone who knew Gaebelein only casually.

*   *   *

As headmaster of a Christian school, he knew that he must surround himself with teachers who would enter wholly into the experience of education that centers upon the Word of God. He agreed with Edwin H. Rian that any philosophy of Christian education "must be rooted in the idea that the foundation of all knowledge is the divine revelation of God in Christ, which can be properly interpreted only by those who have been regenerated by the Spirit of God." He needed a faculty whose lives would exemplify a vital Christian faith. Many persons find this fact about Stony Brook objectionable. Even those who are in friendly disposition toward the teaching of the Bible believe that Frank Gaebelein's *sine qua non* creates too narrow a framework for Christian education. What, then, is the rationale behind the policy of hiring only teachers who profess an active belief in Jesus Christ as Lord?

Joseph Haroutunian has said, "It seems to me to follow that teachers in a Christian school should be Christians, without the least compromise with regard to their professional competence." The typical demurral from this policy, and the usual practice in nominally Christian schools, is stated by Allan Heely, the late headmaster at Lawrenceville, whom Gaebelein deeply respected. In his book, *Why the Private School?*, Heely wrote:

> Those who teach in such schools ought also to include a diversity of religious background; and it is by no means necessary that it should be Christian, though Christian teachers and officials must determine policy and procedure in regard to religion.

On most other matters relating to Christian education, Heely and Gaebelein agreed. For example, the chapter from which this passage is taken is called "The Cornerstone." In this same chapter, Heely speaks of the all-encompassing nature of truth in God and the Christian teacher's opportunity to express that truth.

The fundamental disagreement between these two heads of schools came over their respective attitudes toward the relationship between one's faith and one's apprehension of the truth of God. Frank Gaebelein believes that Jesus Christ bound inextricably a knowledge of Himself and the fullness of truth when He said, "I am the way, the truth, and the life" (John 14:6); he believes that to deny that Jesus Christ is the Truth is to fall into error; he requires that those who take as their motto the words of Jesus, "And ye shall know the truth, and the truth shall make you free," do so in the full context of the passage, which goes on to say, "If the Son therefore shall make you free, ye shall be free indeed" (John 8:32 and 36).

Those who disagree with Frank Gaebelein over the practical business of who should convey the truth *as* God's truth may stand with the writers of the committee report, *General Education in School and College*—the 1952 report by faculty committees representing Andover, Exeter, Lawrenceville, Harvard, Princeton, and Yale. Speaking of their proposed course of study in values, the committee wrote:

> Except in sectarian institutions, we suppose it inevitable that the moral opinions of school and college teachers in this country should be various and even conflicting. Yet we suppose also that these differences surround a considerable area of basic agreement as to what is meant by words like truth and honor. Both the variety and the basic agreement are a part of our age to which students should be exposed.

From Gaebelein's point of view the statements by Allan Heely and by the faculty committee responsible for *General Education in School and College* create irreconcilable contradictions within themselves.

On the one hand, they maintain a sincere concern that the education of the young should include an intellectual familiarity with the Bible. On the other hand, these educators argue that it is reasonable for the Bible to be taught by those who do not necessarily accept it as true for themselves; who do not necessarily accept Jesus Christ as the Truth. Rather, they support the theory that there is strength in the diversity of opinion regarding what the Bible says about the revelation of truth through its pages. Meanwhile *General Education in School and College* expects to find "a considerable area of basic agreement as to what is meant by words like truth and honor," although such an agreed definition cannot be expected to derive from any biblical source.

The paradox, therefore, is baffling and results quite naturally in a headmaster's having to take the defensive posture Dr. Heely strikes when he says, "Teachers in a Christian nonsectarian school, however, may properly be expected and required to assent to its main ethical objectives and to support its religious program as fully as they can." This latter phrase compounds the contradiction, for if such a Christian schoolmaster wishes to develop a religious program that centers about Jesus as the dominant Person of history, the Saviour to whom he has committed his life, he will create a program so Christ-centered as to conflict with the theology or agnosticism of a faculty divided in its degree of Christian commitment. For some who disbelieve altogether the intellectually honest responsibility would be to give no support at all to such a religious program. Therefore, it seems both intellectually incongruous and administratively unsound to suppose that a school can call itself Christian and be in fact a Christian school without adhering to the necessity of a totally united faculty of Christian believers.

This is Joseph Haroutunian's point when he says :

A Christian school that does not work with a Christian understanding of the human enterprise, with the person and work of Christ as its life and energy, that does not engage in the process of education as informed and quickened by the Teacher who is the Spirit of the Father in the Son, is salt without savor and deserves to be thrown away by the Church and forgotten by the people.

So Dr. Gaebelein contends and has contended from his inaugural address. In subsequent statements over the years, the argument has remained unchanged. Writing in the professional journal *Independent Education* for September 1929, he says:

The spiritual power of a school resides not so much in formal religious instructions as in the totality of religious atmosphere. To this, spiritual-minded and sympathetic teachers and a nucleus of high-minded students chiefly contribute.

And in *The Pattern of God's Truth* Dr. Gaebelein devotes a chapter to "The Teacher and the Truth," in which he issues this challenge:

Yes, the crux of the problem lies with the teacher. The fact is inescapable; the world view of the teacher, in so far as he is effective, gradually conditions the world view of the pupil. No man teaches out of a philosophical vacuum. In one way or another, every teacher expresses the convictions he lives by, whether they be spiritually positive or negative.

This is why the school or college that would develop a Christ-centered and Biblically grounded program must fly from its masthead this standard, "No Christian education without Christian teachers," and must never, under any condition, pull its colors down.

One of Gaebelein's critics, Kendig Brubaker Cully, in a chapter on evangelical education, asks the key question:

To staff the ideal Christian school, where would one find adequate numbers of competent scholars to do effective teaching of geography, mathematics, history, etc.?

"Where?" replies Dr. Gaebelein. "Why, from God himself, working in the heart of the teacher to show him that his Christian vocation might be fulfilled at Stony Brook, and working in the hearts of those of us responsible at Stony Brook to recognize that this teacher is God's man to fill the position at this time."

Does this attitude toward hiring mean that the headmaster of a

Christian school takes a passive position, never soliciting candidates for teaching jobs, leaving the entire responsibility to what evangelical Christians call "the leading of the Lord"?

"Not at all," says Dr. Gaebelein. "The responsible administrator must make his needs known to others who are in a position to advise him of an available candidate. God works through men, not through mental telepathy. Let me give you an illustration. A few years ago, I needed to fill a position in English. I also needed a man to conduct our choral music. And I needed someone who could assist in our athletic program. I wrote to a friend, the chairman of the English Department at a leading Christian college, to inquire about any of his graduating English majors whom he might recommend.

"The very day my letter arrived a young man, a graduate fellow teaching Freshman English, stopped by my friend's office to tell him that he had decided, for personal reasons, to look for a position elsewhere. As it happened—I'm sure, in the providence of God— that man was an experienced choir director and an athlete. He came to Stony Brook, feeling with me that God would have him use his background and skills to fill Stony Brook's needs. He has been with us ever since. I didn't apply to a teacher placement bureau, and he didn't take a shot in the dark by writing to me for a job. God brought us together through the friendship and concern of another Christian administrator."

In the spring of 1950, the British chapters of Inter-Varsity Christian Fellowship sent a delegation of young men from Oxford and Cambridge universities to the United States to tour the campuses of schools and colleges. Two members of that team were Peter K. Haile of Oxford and John K. Holmes of Cambridge. On a side trip Haile visited the Stony Brook campus. Some time later, when he was serving as Inter-Varsity's representative among the New England colleges, Peter Haile was invited to Stony Brook for a week of evangelistic meetings. His interest in teaching at the school was quickened, and when he felt directed by God to leave his position with Inter-Varsity, he inquired about a place at Stony Brook. In 1961, Haile was appointed to the faculty, teaching English; in 1963, he became school chaplain.

Meanwhile, his friend John Holmes had gone to West Africa, where he was senior lecturer in mathematics at the University of

Science and Technology, Kumasi, Ghana. During a second
American visit, he came to Stony Brook to see Peter Haile, and in
1969 he returned to join the faculty as a teacher of mathematics and
physics and as an academic counselor. In such a way the providence
of God has directed men to Stony Brook.

"I rarely found it necessary to go hunting for faculty through
teacher agencies or anything of that sort," says Frank Gaebelein.
"In every instance without exception the best teachers Stony Brook
has had have come of their own volition, led I am positive by the
guiding hand of God."

However, neither Frank Gaebelein nor any other schoolmaster
would claim that the staffing of a Christian school—with wholly
committed Christians who are also competent teachers—is a simple
matter. It is often a slow and discouraging process. Over the years
some teachers at Stony Brook have failed to measure up to the
standards by which they were hired. Because it is true that God
works through men, it must also be admitted that men fall short, at
every level, of fulfilling their highest potential. Occasionally, a less
than competent man receives a misleading recommendation from
someone whose notion of kindness does an injustice to the unwary;
or an administrator, sensing a candidate's weakness, hopes
nonetheless that the strength of his more experienced colleagues
will pull the new man through; or a wife, sweet and demure at the
time of the interview, may turn out to be a hindrance in the
boarding-school situation; or a well-meaning man gets off to an
unsatisfactory start from which he does not recover.

One new teacher, full of good intentions and believing that he was
fulfilling the Stony Brook ideal for the integration of all truth as
God's truth, offered an honors grade in his chemistry class to any
boy who would memorize the Gospel according to St. John. His
students, far less naive than he, took him at his word. One boy had
six chapters learned before word leaked to the headmaster and the
class's efforts were redirected to learning the periodic table. The
new man did not last the school year, although he had come with
unusually fine recommendations.

"Why is it," asked a senior boy during a discussion of student-
faculty relationships, "that a boy can tell in ten seconds what an
administrator seems to miss in a two-hour interview, namely the
fact that this man will not command my respect?" It is a hard

question, one which every employer—whether schoolmaster or manufacturer—must answer at some time during his career. When Frank Gaebelein attempts to answer, he shows in his face some of the regret for past mistakes. "I suppose it all comes down to a matter of judgment. We ask the Lord to send us the right man, and three men come. We do our best, using the experience of our years and our common sense, to make the right decision. And we pray. And we ask the candidate to pray for God's guidance too. Then a decision has to be made, and we pick one man over the other two, trusting God that we've chosen wisely. When it turns out that we're wrong, it's a very humbling lesson we learn. It tells us all over again how dependent we must be upon the Lord and not rely alone on our own systems of measurement."

The qualifications for a Stony Brook teacher are, first, an acknowledged Christian commitment and, second, competence in one's academic discipline. But he must also demonstrate two other qualities: he must be manly and he must possess and be able to express a concern and love for teenagers.

Although Stony Brook has become a coeducational school, it continues to be very much a masculine school. To some observers it has been a school in which athletics have been too greatly glamorized to the diminishing of other phases of the curriculum. Certainly the School gives a high place to sports, and it expects its faculty to exhibit a manly appearance and fitness. This is not only because the School benefits from the physical well-being of its faculty but also because the teacher himself will be more successful if he shows a strong constitution. He need not be a "he-man," but he must demonstrate what Dr. Gaebelein calls "force." He means that personal quality that gives a man a firm handshake and a look of self-confidence. This force of character develops a satisfactory relationship between the teacher and his pupils, thereby lessening the number and severity of disciplinary incidents.

A man may have all the other qualities to recommend him as a teacher at Stony Brook, but if he does not love teenaged boys and girls and enjoy working with them in the daily routine of the boarding-school life, he does not qualify. For the young man starting out, unless he is a boarding-school graduate, perhaps the closest parallel experience may have been the job of camp counselor. To some degree, the boarding-school teacher lives for nine months as a camp counselor does for eight weeks—eating, sleeping, working, studying, and playing with a cabin group (in this case, a dormitory). Such a life brings teacher and pupil into proximity; the dormitory becomes a house, and one hopes a home in which the student feels welcome.

But that welcome can sometimes wear thin, as when a corridor rumpus awakens the infant from his nap in the faculty apartment; or when a resident master, not on supervisory duty and relaxing in his quarters, is called to the door for the ninth time and asked, "Sir, are you on duty tonight?" Or when a student, notorious for his indolence throughout the term, decides the night before an examination to apply for special tutoring. These are the tests of a man's patience and good will.

There are also tests of sensitivity and tact. Standing by his campus mailbox in Johnston Hall one day, a young teacher offered a casual greeting to a boy nearby who was about to open a letter. Suddenly the boy, the son of missionaries, convulsed in shock. The letter he was reading, from his grandparents, was to console him on his father's death—a fact which, because of confusion at the mission headquarters, had not yet been conveyed to him or to anyone at Stony Brook. In an instant the teacher found himself shifted in roles from a maker of small talk to the only immediate support available to a stricken boy.

On other occasions the very nature of communal living may lead to a clash of personalities between a man and boy. When the boy is wrong, it may seem an easy thing to correct him and, if necessary, take the proper disciplinary action. But the man's true concern shows itself when he follows up his action, when he seeks out the offender and counsels with him to make certain, not necessarily that the boy likes the man, but that the boy knows the man does not hold the boy's action against him.

The greater test of Christian character and of love for adolescents comes when the teacher has been at fault—when his anger has outweighed its cause, when his accusation has been misdirected, when his pride has been injured. Then his profession of Christian faith is being evaluated as it never is when he is speaking before the School in chapel or lecturing his class on some moral issue. His stature as a man will be measured not by the degree of his fault—for the young are seldom so self-righteous as to deny the possibility of human error—but by the length of time it takes for an adult to own up to his fault and make it right.

The molding of such a faculty to sustain the reputation of a school is not a short-term process. It begins with aspirations embodied in criteria such as those enumerated here—spiritual vitality, scholarship and competent teaching ability, forceful character, and love for young people. It swells and diminishes organically, like any living body, as its members grow in experience, leave, and are replaced by others. One of the marks of a successful school is its contented, although not complacent faculty. If this can be measured by years, it is worth noting that Stony Brook has established a solid corps of teachers who have served for ten years or more—in 1972, twelve men and women. Of this number, two have served fifteen years or more, one for twenty-seven years, and Floyd Johnson, the senior master, for thirty-five years.

The present faculty consists of men and women whose accomplishments are known beyond the boundaries of the Stony Brook campus. The headmaster was recently elected to the Headmasters Association. He has been chairman of the College Entrance Examination Board's committee on entrance procedures; he is on the board of the Council for Religion in Independent Schools and has served on other important educational and civic committees. The senior master has been president of the Ivy Preparatory School League. The chaplain is on the board of the Latin America Mission. The English Department chairman is the College Board's consultant on Advanced Placement in English for the northeastern United States and serves on the Commission on the English Curriculum for the National Council of Teachers of English. At a reading of the College Board's English composition achievement test, out of some one hundred and fifty secondary school readers chosen from all over the country, four were from Stony Brook. Stony Brook teachers are responsible for a series of textbooks on American literature published by a major firm, and for numerous essays, articles, and poems published in professional journals and in the evangelical periodicals. Summer fellowships for graduate study in American history, chemistry, English, foreign languages, mathematics, physics, and counseling have been awarded by the University of California at Berkeley, Franklin and Marshall, Harvard, Knox, New York University, Oberlin, and Princeton, to name only a few.

But as important as these professional distinctions are, even more significant is the respect with which the Stony Brook faculty is held in its own community. In 1968, when the Three Village Junior Chamber of Commerce inaugurated its awards for Outstanding Young Man and Outstanding Young Educator, the two men selected were both teachers at The Stony Brook School. In churches throughout the community, Stony Brook faculty and their families take leading parts. It is a rare Sunday, particularly during the summer months of pastors' vacations, when a Stony Brook teacher-layman is not preaching in a church somewhere on Long Island.

In all these varied pursuits, some directly related to their vocation as teachers and some more broadly defined as Christian responsibilities, Stony Brook's faculty members have had as their example the founding headmaster Dr. Frank E. Gaebelein, who established the high standard, and the one other man who most fully embodied the fulfillment of those standards, Pierson Curtis.

* * *

At the time that John F. Carson and his associates were arranging for the opening of the Stony Brook Assembly's first conference season, a young man named Arthur Pierson Curtis was completing his preparatory schooling at Mount Hermon School.

Like his friend and long-time colleague, Frank Gaebelein, Pierson Curtis also came from a family whose roots ran deeply into evangelical Christian service. His grandfather, Arthur T. Pierson, was one of the great Bible teachers of the nineteenth century, a friend of Moody and of A. J. Gordon. Pierson had within him a passion for foreign missions; his own children shared this passion, including his daughter who married a young theological student and missionary candidate, Frederick Curtis, and went with him to Japan.

In Kobe, their first son was born on March 18, 1889. He was named Arthur Pierson Curtis, for his grandfather. His first schooling was at home, but at the outbreak of the Russo-Japanese War he was sent to the China Inland Mission's school in Chefoo, China.

Pierson Curtis was sixteen years old when he left the Orient for the school in northern Massachusetts. He was stepping into a new world, a world consisting of books he had not yet read. "At that age," says Pierson Curtis, "little else than books mattered to me. I had read and re-read everything available to me in Japan. But here I was with all these modern books just waiting for me to read them. I set about to devour them, at the expense of everything else."

A wise but tough Latin teacher named Miss Bigelow helped show him the priority of his academic responsibilities. She was teaching Cicero, and Curtis was managing to get passing grades with as little effort as possible. At report-card time, Miss Bigelow called him to her desk and gave him a failing grade of 50. He was greatly distressed and pointed out that none of his grades had been low enough to merit the failing mark for that period. "For you, Curtis, there is no grade between 90 and 50," she replied. The dismayed boy, feeling that he had a manifest case of injustice to be resolved in his favor, took his charges to the headmaster Henry F. Cutler. "I was ushered into the headmaster's office. He was a little man with a bald head and glasses, sitting in a swivel chair at his roll-top desk. He turned in his chair and looked over at me and said, 'What is it?' I carefully explained my problem and how I felt I had been wronged in being told that there was no mark for me between 90 and 50. 'What mark did you receive?' Mr. Cutler asked, and I told him. 'That is what you get. Good morning.' That was that. Any word of protest from me, and I would have been on a train away."

But Pierson Curtis left the Mount Hermon headmaster's office that morning a different person. He decided to accept his Latin teacher's challenge. For him, indeed, there would be no acceptable mark between excellence and failure. From that point on, in his studies of language and literature, he received only the highest grades. What is more, when Miss Bigelow found that she had to withdraw from teaching near the end of the next year's course, she recommended to Mr. Cutler that Curtis take over the class. "I never ceased to be thankful for the hard lesson I learned," he says. The lesson is one that was passed on to his own students during more than a half-century of teaching.

At Mount Hermon, Pierson Curtis was known as "Jap," a reference to his foreign birthplace. He was older than most of his classmates, but he felt nonetheless the loneliness of a boy away from home. At Chefoo, he had been one of many missionary sons, and home was really not so far away. His own experience as a schoolboy cultivated in him a remarkable sensitivity for the torment of a homesick boy. He was vigilant throughout a school year but especially so during the terrifying opening weeks when the homesick boy is often baffled by his mixed feelings and ashamed to the point of fear that he will be labeled a "mama's boy." His remedy was to make the disoriented boy feel useful and needed in his new environment.

From Mount Hermon, Pierson Curtis went to Princeton in the fall of 1909, even though the Pierson family had an honorable tradition at Yale, where Abraham Pierson had been president (1701-1707) and Pierson College stands in his memory. At Princeton, Pierson Curtis studied literature and became a reliable middle-distance runner on the Princeton track team, competing in the 880 yards and the mile run. He was not quite in a class with John Paul Jones of Cornell. When Jones set the world's record, at 4:14 minutes, in the Intercollegiates, Curtis was not a contender. He says, with his typical self-effacement and irony, "I had an excellent view of the finish from the rear."

He received his bachelor's degree with admission to Phi Beta Kappa in the spring of 1913. He had prepared to be a teacher of English, and so his long experience in education began at the Kingsley School in Essex Fells, New Jersey. He had appointments at Browne and Nichols and at Pawling schools, and service in the United States Navy before coming to Stony Brook. By 1924, the start of the School's third year, he had accepted an appointment and launched a forty-four-year career.

It took Pierson Curtis only a short time to make his catholic interests and matching abilities useful throughout the School. By 1926, his third year at Stony Brook, he had a portfolio of responsibilities to defy the writing of a job description. He was primarily a teacher of English with classes at the tenth-, eleventh-, and twelfth-grade levels. He also conducted remedial classes in penmanship and spelling. On alternate evenings he had supervisory responsibilities, which he shared with Charles Ruffner in Johnston Hall.

In addition to these responsibilities, Curtis was the librarian, chairman of the Scholarship Committee and therefore responsible for the academic records of the School, and a member of the Scheduling Committee. Beyond these duties he also found time to be faculty advisor to the Carson Literary Society and to assist in the publication of *The Adventurer,* the literary magazine. He further helped with the voluntary Fellowship meeting, a student-led devotional service held every Tuesday night in the headmaster's home.

Curtis still had time to coach tennis and track. But his major outdoors activity was with the Boy Scout troop, which continued as the Outing Club after it disbanded as a formal scouting organization. Every Saturday afternoon—rain or shine—the campers met at one of their select sites for a cook-out. From time to time, overnight camping was included.

The distinguished writer Richard H. Rovere, '33, political columnist for *The New Yorker*, has said of his relationship with Pierson Curtis, "In my earliest memories, he is not a teacher but a Scoutmaster, which was all right with me. At thirteen, I was a reluctant scholar but a most enthusiastic Boy Scout, and he led us on some splendid adventures: camping out in winter at Kings Park and Wading River and in fall and spring working on the hull of an ancient sailboat in Port Jefferson harbor. I don't remember ever sailing in the boat, but I do remember scraping the hull."

In the Outing Club every boy was met on a new and common ground as a man in the out-of-doors. Here was no class ranking on the basis of familiarity with geometry theorems or the conjugation of a Latin verb. What mattered was the boy's willingness to learn how to slough off the conveniences of civilization and adapt himself to working with fewer and more primitive tools. In Pierson Curtis a boy could see an example of the full potential in a liberal education, for here was both the man of letters and the inventor of a reflector oven able to produce, from scratch, biscuits and cakes to rival the finest chef's. Here was also a woodsman and a navigator, a qualified Maine guide, deeply respectful of nature and deeply in communion with the God who had created nature for man to subdue and enjoy.

The new member of the Outing Club soon learned that the club's sponsor was willing to teach camping and cooking skills by demonstration, but he expected the boys thereafter to do the work. A youngster having difficulty keeping rowboat oars in the open oarlock was given a careful explanation of the prescribed technique—including a reasonable account of why the oarlock was open—and then shown on the water how to row efficiently. With the boat tied by a long line, the boy was next sent out to practice what he had been shown before being cut loose to row on his own.

Notices of Outing Club activities appeared on the bulletin boards signed, "P.C." Before long the initials were adopted with as much respect as might ever be accorded "Mr. Curtis." To this day he is still P.C. to those who know him.

As a teacher, Pierson Curtis was never fancy or faddish. He loved the English language and its principal poets: Shakespeare, Milton, Keats, and Shelley. Among the novelists his favorites were Dickens, Hardy, and Conrad. He felt that most boyish aversions to poetry resulted from an unnatural prissiness in the teacher's introduction of a poem—a false sense of seriousness about the business of reading a poem that soon became a precious fondling. P.C. preferred to grapple with a poem, to treat it like a living thing of beauty, but he deplored the attitude that ever suggested mastery of a work of art. "The silliest thing a boy can say about a piece of literature is, 'Oh, I *covered* that last year.' Too bad for him."

P.C. believed that an educated man maintained a steady diet of reading, and he was always ready with a book to recommend and hand to a student or colleague. One of his favorite writers was Kenneth Roberts, whose *Northwest Passage* and *Arundel* were frequently being passed around by P.C.'s proteges. Among the Christian writers his favorites were C. S. Lewis, Dorothy Sayers, and Alan Paton. Lewis's books, in particular *Perelandra,* and Paton's *Cry, the Beloved Country* are still a part of Stony Brook's English syllabus, since being introduced by P.C. twenty years ago.

P. C. demanded clarity in his students' writing. He recognized the tendency among schoolboys to affect a literary pose when putting pen to paper. Richard Rovere recalls how P. C.'s criticism followed him to college: "He was the first person to give me what is just about the most valuable thing a writer can have—an aversion to fattiness to prose. He drilled it into us in school, and I remember an extra lick when I was almost through college. I was the editor of the college paper, and he came to our campus to visit. He picked up a copy of the paper I was editing, read some stuffy and didactic editorial of mine, put it down and said, 'There is no such word as *thusly*.' "

A former colleague, Dr. J. Wesley Ingles, remembers an incident with his son, Bruce Ingles, '53. Apparently young Ingles had developed a flamboyance in his writing that his father—himself a novelist and later Professor of English at Eastern Baptist College—wished to eradicate. "He was getting A's from his teacher, which dismayed me because I could see the pruning that was needed. Entering his senior year, Bruce was assigned to another teacher, not to Pierson Curtis. I was disturbed. One of the most important experiences I wanted for him at Stony Brook was Senior English with P. C. I appealed and graciously the School transferred him to P. C.'s class. As I had expected, his grades dropped at once from A's to C's. He wasn't happy about the change, but I was and told him why. By the year's end he had pulled himself together, learned to write well, and tied for the English prize."

As Pierson Curtis grew older and his coaching duties ceased, he made himself available every afternoon in the period between the end of athletics and the call for dinner. Boys in deep academic difficulty were assigned to study at this time, and they called themselves "P. C.'s 5:30 Honor Roll." Their tutor belonged to an age before the overspecialization of teaching reduced most teachers to a single ken. P. C. seemed to have taken all knowledge to be his province. He could help them in algebra or geometry, in French, Spanish, or Latin; in history, Bible, or English. Many a man today can recall how, as afternoon shadows darkened, he used to hear the stern, yet loving voice, of the senior master at his shoulder saying, "Yes, General, but you forgot that the verb *to be* always takes the nominative case."

They were all "General." And he was P. C. and taught boys how to think through a fog of unreasonable argument and into the rhetoric of truth. He knew what Gilbert Highet means when he says, "To teach a boy the difference between truth and lies in print, to start him thinking about the meaning of poetry or patriotism, to hear him hammering back at you with the facts and arguments you have helped him to find, sharpened by himself and fitted to his own powers, gives the sort of satisfaction that an artist has when he makes a picture out of blank canvas and chemical colorings, or a doctor when he hears a sick pulse pick up and carry the energies of new life under his hands."

P. C.'s classes were no more memorable than his chapel talks—never sermons but often storytellings with Pierson Curtis leaning over the pulpit, caught up in the mystery and the miracle of the narrative as his words unraveled it. Young men who may have become glazed or hardened by an overdose of homilies in daily chapel could scarcely turn off a Bible story narrated by so masterly a storyteller. He would relate, for instance, the handwriting on the wall or another of his favorites, the story of Esther, her kinsman Mordecai, and the evil schemer Haman. As the intrigue unwound to its ironic conclusion, P. C.'s audience would be caught as if in stop-film, with none of the foot-shuffling and bench-creaking that so often marks that teenaged audience. At his prayer, now leaning out over the pulpit, arms crossed upon his chest, Pierson Curtis's devotion to Christ and love for his audience were blended as one.

He was not a man whose relationship with the young made up for some lack of warmth toward adults. But he seemed to possess that special charm which made him the friend of little children. In the dining room after a meal, his table was the center of children's entertainment. He was nobody's Mr. Chips, he was everybody's P. C. Toward the younger couples on the faculty he was especially kind, serving as household photographer for special occasions such as the arrival home of a newborn and its mother, or with his wife, Dr. Winifred Woodman Curtis, opening their home at Bailey Island to them for a week's vacation on the delightful Maine coast.

As the senior master, he was both a leader of the faculty and a loyal supporter of the administration. When a teacher needed either encouragement or reprimand, it was given without either sentimentality or bitterness. A Down Easter by preference, Pierson Curtis knew the value of brevity both in commendation and rebuke. He would speak with sincerity and with evident earnestness and then take his leave.

* * *

The nature of man is such that he needs to share his responsibilities. Melville's Captain Ahab rejected this need and cursed "this mortal interindebtedness." Yet sane men know that to attend any major human enterprise without the benefit of counsel and the sharing of burdens is to court grave risk. A wife can help; yet she is seldom sufficient for such circumstances. A man needs a comrade, a partner in his labors in whom to confide and with whom to face each day's new problems. In the providence of God, few great men fail to find such a friend, a Jonathan to their David.

In his experience at Stony Brook, through the School's founding years, Frank Gaebelein had known the encouragement and trust of men like John Carson and Ford Ottman, he had gained the respect of the older and more experienced members of his faculty, and he had found and married a wife from whom he gained love and consolation. But it can scarcely be said that he had a friend, a comrade, at Stony Brook until he came to know and appreciate Pierson Curtis.

The development of their friendship was cautious and temperate, for they had many differences that could have resulted in their disunity had it not been for that deepening commitment to the purposes of Stony Brook. Gaebelein carried himself with the air of patrician superiority, while Curtis seemed more a commoner. Gaebelein was aggressive, demanding, sometimes imperious; Curtis could be blunt and direct but was more often tactful, less likely to offend. Gaebelein was efficient and methodical, the careful executive; Curtis was a reluctant desk man, perfectly able to recall lengthy passages of poetry yet not at all sure where he had placed a memorandum. Both were dedicated outdoorsmen, yet here too their preferences differed, for Gaebelein was a mountaineer and a fisherman, while Curtis was a wilderness camper and sailor. Gaebelein was an accomplished musician, but Curtis was a painter working in water colors.

They came together in their love of God and their devotion to serve Him by serving boys. Each had consecrated his life to the Christian ministry through education; each had chosen to make that ministry in the sphere of preparatory schooling rather than college or seminary education. Frank Gaebelein had molded a living school out of the ideas and theories of its founders; Pierson Curtis had seen in that school the values and opportunities he favored. This became their bond.

Reading their correspondence from 1924, one comes upon a letter from the headmaster that is a landmark in their experience and, consequently, in the experience of the School. It is a routine business letter, dated July 13, 1927, but it begins with the salutation, "My dear Pierson." Previously he had been "My dear Mr. Curtis." The reply is in equal terms of friendship, without any diminishing of respect for the office he addressed. Throughout their remaining years at Stony Brook, these two men maintained both the intimacy of their friendship and their mutual understanding of authority. When they disagreed, as they sometimes did over a matter of policy or the continuation of a student or faculty member, they could express themselves strongly yet with the restraint of gentlemen who respected each other. So their bond strengthened.

It was a bond renewed often through prayer. To whatever degree these two men differed in temperament and in style, they became as one in the force of their prayer together. They are men who believe in the efficacy of prayer, and they met often to pray together or with other colleagues at regularly convened times such as Tuesday mornings before breakfast in Johnston Hall, Wednesday evenings in Hegeman Chapel, and after Sunday service in the headmaster's study. For many years they shared together a brief time of Bible reading and prayer each week. Their correspondence, particularly during the summer months of separation when one was at Stony Brook and the other at camp in Maine, contains many instances of mutual encouragement and requested prayer—prayer for wisdom in the making of decisions, prayer for specific boys and men, prayer for the financial needs of the School.

Dr. Gaebelein was always jealous for the dignity of secondary school teaching. A teacher contemplating leaving Stony Brook for a college position would run head-on into a lecture on the importance of preparatory school education and its opportunities. The head-master could always point to respected scholars in the man's discipline who had excelled while teaching in a boys' boarding school—the restless English teacher would be reminded that Thornton Wilder had written *The Bridge of San Luis Rey* while teaching at Lawrenceville; that Emily Dickinson's great biographer and cataloguer, Thomas A. Johnson, was a teacher at Lawren-ceville; that the distinguished critic Edmund Fuller and the novelist Frederick Buechner teach at boys' schools. The teacher often left the interview shaken in his decision to "move up," as he may have thought, to higher education, particularly if Frank Gaebelein had also fixed his eye on the man and warned him of the pride of being called "Professor So-'n'-So."

Gaebelein did not disparage college teaching or any other level of teaching. He simply did not agree that the secondary school teacher should stand in awe of the university professor. He knew that Henry Adams had been right when he said, "A teacher affects eternity; he can never tell where his influence stops," and Gaebelein believed this to be as applicable to the preparatory teacher as to the college professor. He agreed with Erasmus, whom he quoted, in *Christian*

Education in a Democracy, in concluding his chapter on teachers:

> To be a schoolmaster is next to being a king. Do you count it a mean employment to imbue the minds of your fellow-citizens in their earliest years with the best literature and with the love of Christ, and to return them to their country honest and virtuous men? In the opinions of fools it is a humble task, but in fact it is the noblest of occupations.

In Pierson Curtis, Erasmus's description of the Christian teacher was given shape, and it was these virtues Frank Gaebelein saw in him and admired. When he wished to outline the qualities of the Christian teacher in his book, *The Pattern of God's Truth,* Dr. Gaebelein drew an image readily familiar to those who also knew Pierson Curtis:

> At this point, I speak from personal experience. For many years I have worked in daily fellowship with a skilled teacher of English. His knowledge of literature is of a breadth and depth possessed by few university professors. His classes provide an experience upon which every graduate of the school where he teaches looks back with appreciation. There is no question of this man's professional competence; when he teaches Shakespeare or Milton, he does so with authority born of long and loving familiarity with their works. And all the time there is another book in which, because he is a devoted Christian, he lives in a sense different from his devotion to the English classics. Not only is his heart in the Bible; through his daily use and constant study of it, the Bible has literally formed his mind. Such a man does not make brief journeys from English literature to the Bible. Despite his constant handling of literature, his true intellectual and spiritual home is in the Word of God. Nor is he any less competent in English because of this fact. Rather is his teaching of a so-called secular subject enriched, because he comes to it with a genuinely Christian world view. Such a man indulges in no forced "reconciliations" between English and Christianity; instead there is in his teaching a natural communication of Christian allusions and attitudes, flowing from a mind and personality steeped in the Bible.

"I think of the statement made by that great Christian statesman, Charles Habib Malik, former President of the General Assembly of the United Nations," says Dr. Gaebelein. 'Find the good teacher and forget everything else.' It's hyperbolic, of course, but those of us who have been charged with the administration of a school—especially a Christian school—know very well what Malik means."

Two men so different in temperament and in style, working together with the help of many others for thirty-nine years, created Stony Brook School. Neither Frank Gaebelein nor Pierson Curtis had in himself the qualities sufficient to satisfy the School's needs; together, however, they complemented each other's strengths to forge the very leadership such a school must have. They also provided, by their joint example, the sure foundation of Christian faith and productive scholarship.

4

Days of Testing, Years of Growth

Any school begun in the early years of this century faced, before its maturity had been achieved, vicissitudes sufficient to cause the school's collapse. First came the Great Depression, stifling growth and causing some schools—even those with an apparently secure financial backing—to resort to high pressure promotion and a lowering of standards to remain solvent. Package-deal admissions to include candidates whose only qualification was the ability to pay were not uncommon. In some schools credit meant more than credentials. The cheapening of a diploma seemed a small price to pay to keep the school alive. Even so, many such schools expired in the thirties.

No sooner had the financial crises ceased than World War II began to decimate faculties and lure away schoolboys to paths of glory. Still later, in the aftermath of war, came a lethargy among some leaders amounting to a failure of nerve.

The years from 1922 to 1963 were often trying for Stony Brook; yet they were also years of stabilization and advancement. At his retirement in 1963, Dr. Gaebelein could look back over forty-one years and say,

> It was Hudson Taylor who said, "God's work done in God's way will not lack God's support." To you of this Board and to my successor I say that this is true. I know it to be true from the experience of forty years. Therefore, as Stony Brook faces the future, let us do as the last chapter of Acts tells us Paul did when, coming to Rome, "he thanked God and took courage." Let us thank God for His goodness to Stony Brook, and let us take heart for the future.

* * *

Saddened by the death of its founder, John F. Carson, just a few days before the term reconvened, Stony Brook nonetheless opened for its sixth year in September 1927. Frank Gaebelein and his faculty of eight now had a student body of about one hundred boys. They came from fourteen states and from Argentina, Burma, Canada, China, Cuba, and Egypt. The School consisted of all twelve elementary and secondary grades, divided into Lower School (grades one to seven) and Upper School (grades eight to twelve). The curriculum in the Upper School offered Bible and English for all; five levels of Latin and three of French; New Testament Greek; ancient, modern, and American history; biology and chemistry; algebra, plane and solid geometry; and business principles. The emphasis was clearly on the humanities, as the headmaster had promised it would be.

To accommodate an expanding student body, new buildings were being constructed, and a memorial campaign fund to finance Carson Hall was already underway. The two newest buildings were a combined classroom-dormitory and a chapel, presented by the estate of John Rogers Hegeman, late president of the Metropolitan Life Insurance Company. At Hegeman's death, Frederick H. Ecker, a Christian layman and member of Dr. Carson's church, was named executor of the estate. Hegeman's will directed that funds be set aside for the construction of buildings at worthy institutions. Having heard often from his pastor about Stony Brook, Ecker directed that the Hegeman estate should provide the young school with the funds to erect the buildings so sorely needed. A similar gift was presented to Brown University.

The proposed Carson Hall was to be a major building, an impressive structure that would accommodate nearly three hundred boarding students, as well as providing additional facilities such as infirmary quarters. The appeal for funds was broadly based, for John Fleming Carson was a familiar name in religious circles and the Stony Brook reputation was growing year by year.

By 1928, almost $150,000 had been contributed and pledged. One of the factors cited by donors themselves as attracting them to give was the School's continuing scholarship program. In the same year that Stony Brook was soliciting funds for the Carson Memorial

Fund, twenty boys were receiving tuition grants amounting to $14,000 on a tuition rate of $850 annually. Few preparatory schools could point to a comparable program in proportion to enrollment and budget. Prospective contributors saw that Stony Brook intended to make its unique Christian education available to boys of all classes, regardless of the parents' ability to pay.

The black days of October 1929 sent the nation into pandemonium, but the immediate groundshock felt elsewhere was not so immediately severe in boarding schools. Tuitions had been paid, supplies had been purchased. But obviously the time was not propitious to press for the completion of the Carson Memorial Fund. With some men standing on bread lines and others leaping out skyscraper windows, the plans for Carson Hall were set aside. The money already at hand pledged for the purpose built a two-story infirmary. In addition, the summer conference auditorium was eventually rehabilitated as a gymnasium with a basement dug out from under the structure to provide for a heating unit and locker rooms. The building was renamed the John F. Carson Memorial Auditorium and Gymnasium and dedicated as such in 1936.

This reduction in a memorial to the School's founder, from a building of truly imposing scope to a refurbished gymnasium, troubled Frank Gaebelein. "Humanly speaking," he says, "it was a lasting disappointment that we were unable to construct a more appropriate memorial to Dr. Carson. But God, in His providence, knew what our needs were. He also knew that we would hardly need facilities for 300 boys when the economy could scarcely provide us with 100. Much as we might have wished for it, the proposed Carson Hall would have been a white elephant for many years."

When the depression economy tightened its grip upon Stony Brook, the faculty was called upon to show its depth of commitment to the School's ideal in a most practical way. To keep the School operating within reasonably solvent conditions, each teacher was asked to accept a graduated reduction in cash salary, exclusive of other boarding school perquisites.

"We began to feel the pinch," Wesley Ingles recalls from his experience at Stony Brook, "and it affected some people's attitudes in quite an adverse manner. There was a good deal of griping in some quarters, especially because the School kept up its practice of giving scholarship aid, in spite of the financial shortage. Of course, there were problems. Needed repairs could be patched at best, and there were many luxuries we felt deprived of. But, you know, those of us who found time to pray together also found that we were supporting each other in morale and in goodwill."

The faculty did pray together, and groups of boys prayed. Informal prayer has been characteristic of Stony Brook life since the School's founding. Dr. Cary N. Weisiger, III, a graduate in the Class of 1927, now pastor of the Menlo Park (California) Presbyterian Church, says that one of his most important recollections from Stony Brook days is "the brief devotional period each morning just before breakfast. We called it 'Morning Watch.' A group of us, sometimes with a faculty member, sometimes without, had a time of Bible reading and prayer; nothing formal. Just some young men telling God that they were giving this day into his charge. This, more than any other experience, helped to shape my Christian growth." During the Depression, these prayers among the faculty became a bond of unity that petitioned God to sustain a School that many felt had been brought into being for his glory.

Wesley Ingles says, "I always came away from prayer with a colleague—after calling upon God's intervention—with an assurance that what we were trying to do at Stony Brook wasn't in vain."

Stony Brook's financial condition in the early stages of the Depression was helped by the presence of Gilbert C. Moore, Sr., the School's first experienced fiscal officer. Appointed by the Stony Brook Assembly, his position included supervision of the summer conference program until his retirement in 1952.

Gilbert Moore recalls his first impressions of Stony Brook's bookkeeping methods: "It's a wonder that the School had lasted the six-and-a-half years it had, with its accounts in such disarray. I learned that the custom had been to telephone the bank and ask what the current balance was, before someone wrote a check against the School's name. In the desk I was given I found little bundles of cash here and a roll of coins there. The School had a deficit of about $20,000. In the first year, simply by more efficient accounting, and by adopting some necessary economies, we cut that sum substantially."

Not only were Stony Brook's accounts in question, but so too were the property rights. John Carson's acquisition of land plots in the name of the Stony Brook Assembly had not always been ac-companied by accurate surveys. Gilbert Moore remembers the chaos: "Not long after I came to Stony Brook, I inquired about buying the house which I was then renting. My wife and I spent most of a day in the county offices in Riverhead going through old deeds and plot maps. You can't imagine how informal the meets and bounds were—'from this oak tree to that clump of bushes, and so forth.' Why, even as late as 1939, we discovered that what we thought was part of our athletic field in fact belonged to a neigh-boring resident. He rightly demanded that either we stop using his property or else pay a rental for it. Fortunately, we were able to buy the piece of land outright and thus end the question of en-croachment.

"At the time, of course, Stony Brook was still a quiet little town. Why, there seemed to be lots of open space around us. Little could we imagine how things would change! How fortunate we were to secure that piece of property—with gifts such as the strip of land behind the headmaster's house, which Dorothy Gaebelein's mother purchased and gave to the Assembly."

In spite of the Depression and its problems, Stony Brook's academic work received growing recognition. In 1930, Stony Brook received a charter from The *Cum Laude* Society, the honor society which most closely corresponds among preparatory schools to Phi Beta Kappa. At the time of Stony Brook's admission, only sixty other schools were members of *Cum Laude*. Admitted along with Stony Brook were Mercersburg Academy, Haverford School, and Kent School.

Membership in *Cum Laude* at Stony Brook is more than an academic distinction. The Society's motto is the Greek words meaning "excellence, justice, honor." To be elected a candidate must have demonstrated that these precepts are inherent in his character.

Stony Brook's reputation as a college preparatory school was enlarging as graduates spread out to colleges and universities across the country. By the end of its tenth year, Stony Brook had graduated more than 150 boys, who had entered some fifty colleges and universities. The Association of Colleges and Secondary Schools of the Middle States had published its first listing of ac-credited schools. Stony Brook had been included, thereby confirming the recognition already accorded by the University of the State of New York in 1923.

In another instance, Stony Brook received unusual recognition. In 1931, Dean Radcliffe Heermance, Director of Admissions at Princeton, commended the School's work in general but cited the Bible courses in particular. He wrote the headmaster that Princeton's admissions committee would willingly accept the study of Bible at Stony Brook as equal to one Carnegie unit of preparation for college. This was an unprecedented acknowledgment of the validity of a rigorous Bible course in preparatory school.

* * *

As if to encourage the faculty further, the students in the early thirties seemed to be unusually mature and gifted. Foremost among them stood Bruce Finlay Vanderveer, '31. "Bud" Vanderveer had transferred to Stony Brook from Mercersburg Academy in the fall of 1929. His older brother had died during the previous school year at Mercersburg, and Bud was too stricken by his death to return to school there. In just two years at Stony Brook he created a remarkable record in his studies and in sports.

"He was a fine combination of athlete and student—a serious student," Wesley Ingles recalls. "I can remember him, stopping after class to talk with me about some of Milton's poems. I remember discussing 'Lycidas' with him, which was particularly ironic, in light of what happened to him. He was the kind of boy who would do that—stop to talk about ideas, when other athletes were tearing to get out of there and off to their sport."

Vanderveer played center on the football team, wrestled, and played tennis. He was an honor student, earning election to The *Cum Laude* Society and receiving at his commencement a citation from the faculty for excellence of character.

From Stony Brook, Bud Vanderveer went on to Harvard. He tried out for crew, even though he had never rowed competitively, because he loved the water (at home he sailed in races on Long Island Sound). Not unexpectedly, Vanderveer made the Harvard freshman crew; not unexpectedly, he was then elected captain of his team.

The next summer, just before returning to Harvard for his sophomore year, Bud Vanderveer piloted his yacht, the Bandit II, to successive championships in Star fleet competition. In the third race of the International Series, he won by more than eight minutes, defeating twenty-seven other contestants. There was no doubt in the minds of spectators and yachting experts that Bruce Vanderveer would be a world champion in just a few days.

But it was not to be. On the day after his qualifying triumph, September 20, 1932, Bud Vanderveer was killed while riding as a passenger in a speeding automobile. The death of this young sportsman had an astonishing effect upon people who knew him and many who did not. For example, the editor of a popular magazine, *Literary Digest,* Arthur S. Draper, wrote a tribute to him.

"In many respects," says Dr. Ingles, "Bud Vanderveer represented some of the finest qualities that Stony Brook wanted to develop in her students."

These qualities are still honored and remembered. The International Star Class Yacht Racing Association awards a cup in Bud Vanderveer's memory to the winner of the third race of the International Series. At Harvard the outstanding member of the freshman crew receives a trophy named for Bud Vanderveer. At Stony Brook the Bruce Finlay Vanderveer Trophy is awarded annually to the football player who has shown the highest qualities of sportsmanship. Bud Vanderveer's Harvard oar hangs in the foyer of Carson Gym.

But there were also other young men of the time of whom Stony Brook could be justly proud. John Warren Hershey, '31, a leading student and athlete while at Stony Brook, then at Franklin and Marshall College in Lancaster, Pennsylvania, saved a woman from an armed attacker by overcoming him and holding him until the police arrived. For his act of bravery Hershey received a Carnegie Medal. In time Hershey would return to Stony Brook as a teacher of English and disciplinary counselor. For more than twenty years the influence of his character and quiet courage were evident, though few of his students knew the story of his bravery.

Others were continuing the pattern, established at Stony Brook, of scholarly attainment in their colleges and universities. At Princeton, Joseph Free and Eric Kocher, both from the Class of 1928, were preparing for distinguished careers that would take them into the widely separated fields of archaeology and diplomacy. Free has contributed to the knowledge of life in the ancient Near East by his expeditionary diggings, particularly at the Old Testament site of Dothan. Kocher spent a quarter-century in the Foreign Service and is now an administrator at the School of International Affairs of Columbia University. At Wheaton College, Robert P. Glover, '31, was preparing for medical school and for his pioneer work in open heart surgery, cut short by his death in 1961.

Meanwhile in the senior class at Stony Brook was a young man named Kenneth Scott who would also gain recognition as a surgeon. His classmates regarded him as something of a "grind"—once when a power shortage dimmed the lights in Hegeman Hall, Scott was found standing on a chair in the corridor, a textbook held up to the barely glowing electric bulb in order to finish his homework. His earnestness would bear fruit, however, in his work as a Presbyterian missionary doctor. He became widely known for his development of successful prostheses for amputees in Korea and India. Today Dr. Scott is president of the Christian Medical College and Brown Memorial Hospital in Ludhiana, India.

Of course, Stony Brook also had its share of the typical teenagers of the period—interested in sports, girls, aviation, popular music, and always on the hunt for a new loophole in the regulations. Among the most enterprising in this latter regard was a group of seniors in the Class of 1933, headed by Frederick Robinson and Ledley Perrin. According to Perrin, someone in the class had discovered that, in one of the Prohibition rulings, the courts had decided that 3.2 beer was not intoxicating. Stony Brook's handbook declared that "the use of intoxicating beverages is forbidden." This was the very loophole these boys had been looking for!

"On the day the ruling was announced," Perrin, a member of Stony Brook's board of trustees, recalls, "a majority of the senior class strolled down to the village, purchased one or two bottles of 3.2 each, along with a supply of pretzels, and prepared for a party. By prearrangement the meeting place was my room on the third floor of Hegeman Hall. After study hours that night, the law-abiding scofflaws gathered there, each with his bottles and pretzels under his jacket or shirt.

"Behind closed doors dozens of bottles were opened—most of us,

I'm sure, for the first time pouring heads of beer. We didn't even know enough *not* to shake well before using! It wasn't long before the overflowing beer gave the room a genuine pub aroma, which lasted, by the way, until commencement.

"The master on dormitory duty that night was J. Wesley Ingles, a fine teacher but with very strict· standards regarding temperance. His thick glasses gave him a stern, ultra-serious appearance. As he made the room check, he knocked on our door, and I said innocently, 'Come in.' I'll never forget the astounded, sterner-than-ever expression as he opened that door and exposed himself completely to that sinful scene."

The next day was spent in a series of faculty conferences, while the administration struggled to close the gap between Stony Brook's rules and the Supreme Court's judgment. "In those distant times," Ledley Perrin continues, "chapel services were held after supper, so there was a whole day of senior and faculty uncertainty. Finally, the whole School came together in the chapel. There sat Gaebie, as usual on the right-hand throne, towering above us seniors in the front rows, his eyes and nose more eagle-like than ever. When time came for the announcements, he arose with a stern demeanor to advise us that the rules of the School now read, 'The use of intoxicating beverages *and beer* is forbidden.'

"No *Te Deum* ever rang out with the joy of our chapel recessional that night, as we smirked down the aisle! We had brought down the administration!"

There were also the eccentrics, those who stood out from the rest of the students for one reason or another. Richard H. Rovere, '33, has portrayed one of these in his story, "Wallace," based on a Stony Brook schoolmate. Wallace Duckworth is the prototype of the "scientifical genius." According to Rovere's tale, Wallace decides to "twitch up" the organ in the chapel. When the Sunday morning service is about to begin, the headmaster and the organist discover that the organ won't function. Wallace, naturally, "untwitches" the organ, much to the expressed delight of all concerned—particularly Wallace. All this is apocryphal, but Rovere does include the prank of the real Wallace Duckworth, who did indeed pour sugar into Coach Ruffner's gasoline tank. Ruffner's car, filled with his basketball team, stalled on the way to an important game. Shortly thereafter the real Wallace Duckworth was expelled.

* * *

The Depression deepened and income grew less and less, enrollment had fallen to barely one hundred boys, and Dr. Gaebelein was often criticized for insisting that students who could pay the tuition should nonetheless be of worthy character. One year, for example, five boys whose tuition could have been paid in full were not invited to return to the School because, Dr. Gaebelein felt, "their influence had been detrimental." At the same time, Stony Brook was endeavoring to survive and still offering more than $13,000 worth of tuition grants to students who would not otherwise have been able to attend.

"I'm positive that God honored our continuing to give scholarship aid," Dr. Gaebelein says. "How else could this little school have continued? We had almost no endowment whatsoever. We could barely pay our bills; often we had to borrow against our good name. Yet when the Depression ended, Stony Brook had been brought through."

How was this possible?

"The scholarship program at Stony Brook," says Frank Gaebelein, "is a clear fulfillment of the Scripture's promise, 'Cast your bread upon the waters, for you will find it after many days.' I couldn't begin to list the men—some of them today in highly influential positions as ministers, teachers, heads of corporations— whom we were able to help financially. In by far the majority of cases, it has been money well spent."

Stony Brook participates in the College Entrance Examination Board's School Scholarship Service. This agency determines the financial capabilities of an applicant's parents, based upon confidential records. When the application has been completed, the director of admissions, in consultation with the headmaster, awards a certain percentage of the tuition to the most desirable and needy candidates.

Except for those students who are recipients of memorial scholarships awarded on merit, the names of scholarship holders are not known generally throughout the School, either by faculty or students. At one time the daily Work Program was conducted exclusively by scholarship holders; some previous admissions officers also assigned the least desirable rooms to students receiving the largest grants. Happily, in both cases a more enlightened policy of Christian benevolence and democratic community life now prevails. Living quarters are assigned without regard for scholarship status by persons who do not even know whether or not a student is receiving financial aid.

A scholarship holder at Stony Brook may, however, be asked into the headmaster's office and reminded of his obligations if his academic work or deportment should fall below a satisfactory level. "We don't nag these people," says Donn Gaebelein, "or make them feel that we're constantly looking over their shoulders. But a teenager needs to know that he or she is accountable for somebody's investment of a thousand dollars or so. There's a responsibility to be maintained here, and we try to maintain it."

Stony Brook survived the 1929 Depression because many people were willing to sacrifice themselves and risk their money to keep the School alive. For instance, the faculty's reduced salaries amounted to almost $35,000 in the years 1932 to 1939. But the School also survived because it was headed by a man of abiding faith in the God who had called Stony Brook into being. "During those years the promises of God in the Scriptures, especially the promises of His faithfulness, became especially precious to me," says Dr. Gaebelein. "A statement like Paul's to the Thessalonian Christians—'Faithful is he that calleth you, who also will do it'—brought us the assurance that we needed day after day."

Frank Gaebelein believed that God had ordained Stony Brook, had blessed Stony Brook in its early years. He believed now that God would sustain the School. This faith, matched by the faithfulness of his fellow workers, kept Stony Brook from the abyss into which so many other institutions fell during that direful time.

*   *   *

According to some economists, the American Depression that started with the Wall Street collapse in October 1929 was ended by the blitzkreig assaults of Adolf Hitler on September 1, 1939. Whether valid or not as a political-economic generalization, it is certainly true that the first year of World War II was also Stony Brook's first year of financial reprieve from the succession of losses. In 1939, the School showed a balance for the first time in the decade; salary reductions were partially restored; long-standing unpaid accounts were settled. The financial state of the School was surely improving.

By 1941, Stony Brook had achieved its peak enrollment at 141 boys. Just as quickly, however, the Day of Infamy at Pearl Harbor brought upon Stony Brook a new set of complications fully as taxing as those of the previous decade. In the fall of 1942, enrollment had slipped back to 117. "Things in education were in a state of nation-wide confusion," Dr. Gaebelein recalls. "Only military schools seemed to find no difficulty with enrollment. Parents who might have sent their sons to school in peacetime now wanted to have them at home. The lowering of the draft eligibility began to affect older boys in school, and even some of the professional agencies, such as the National Education Association, were suggesting that secondary schooling be cut at three years. It was a time of great struggle because one always had to keep the good of the nation in mind, as well as the good of the School."

To enlarge its enrollment base, the School returned to admitting younger boys for fifth and sixth grades. But enrollment was not the most severe problem; getting and keeping qualified faculty became more and more difficult. Major John Lynch Davis, the newly appointed assistant headmaster, was recalled to active duty. Five other men were drafted; still others were expecting to be called.

"We knew that a boys' school must have men teachers," says Dr. Gaebelein. "We were able to prevail upon several local pastors, who came to help us."

Stony Brook made adjustments in the curriculum to reflect the national priorities in a time of war. A course in aeronautics was now being offered; athletic exercise included running through a junior commando course, complete with the scaling of an eight-foot wall; and there was military drill. Stony Brook was taking the war seriously. In the October 1942 issue of *The Blue and White,* the student magazine, Dr. Gaebelein addressed the student body in a combination of patriotic and headmasterly rhetoric:

> What can Stony Brook do to help win the war? That is the question before us this year. Schools are more and more being called upon to do their part in the all-out effort America and her allies are making. . . .
>
> This article is not written to discuss details; there is opportunity for that elsewhere. It aims rather to make just one vital point. As never before, your masters are busy. Faculty changes because of the war, planning for

new courses, revision of schedules—these and similar responsibilities require time for thought and preparation. Therefore, *the greatest contribution the student body can make right now is to develop a stronger sense of responsibility.* When important work is to be done, it is unpatriotic for boys to indulge in childish fooling so as to waste the time of teacher and pupil alike in dealing with these matters. . . .

As a Christian School we have a testimony to maintain. And an essential part of our testimony is to support and work for our country. Stony Brook, let's do our part!

"Some of our older boys were eager—as you might expect from young men—to prove their manhood and courage by getting right into the armed services," Dr. Gaebelein recalls. "For a time it seemed that scarcely a day went by that some boy didn't tell me that he wanted to leave school and sign up, and he wanted my encouragement to help convince his parents that it was the patriotic thing to do. Of course, I could understand how they felt because I felt somewhat the same myself."

Frank Gaebelein wished to enlist in the chaplain's corps, but he would not leave Stony Brook in uncertain hands. Several men were approached about taking the position of acting headmaster, but none accepted. Pierson Curtis did not wish the job either. Gaebelein was deeply disappointed, but he saw, too, that his present work was not unrelated to the total national effort.

Frank Gaebelein remained at Stony Brook. There had been previous opportunities to go elsewhere—administrative positions in college or seminary; there would be more such invitations in the future. But his life's work was to be principally at Stony Brook.

*   *   *

The first effects of the war upon the School were related to personnel—enrollment, faculty, enlistments, and the draft. But there were also problems with equipment and supplies. The plant had not been kept up during the Depression simply because of insufficient funds to make any but major repairs. The buildings needed refurbishing. Classroom materials such as blackboards and desks needed to be replaced. Now, however, many of these supplies were simply not available to the domestic consumer. Paper shortage made textbooks scarce.

"We learned to make do with what we had," says the present

senior master, Floyd Johnson, "and we never threw away a sheet of paper just because it had writing on one side. We turned it over and used the other side."

With the imposition of food rationing, Stony Brook began to face a severe problem in obtaining sufficient quantities of proper food.

"With food rationing so tight, we requested that boys bring the stamps allotted to them to school, but few did that," Gilbert Moore recalls. "So Frank Gaebelein and I had to resort to every possible means of getting enough food for one hundred and more growing boys. Some of our friends were very helpful in those difficult days. For example, I knew a man on the South Shore who had a duck farm, and I could go over there and fill the trunk of my car with Long Island duck!

"Our trustee, John Adams Henry, had a food purveying business, and he was able to supply us with extra stamps. And then a baking company that also manufactured meat pies provided us with ration coupons.

"One day," Moore continues, "I went in early to the Washington Market in New York to meet a contact who, I was told, could get us some meat. I waited for most of the morning, and at last out came a man pulling a cartload of various cuts of meat, and calling out 'Stony Brook Hospital, Stony Brook Hospital.' I went over to him and introduced myself and said, 'But I'm from the Stony Brook School, not Stony Brook Hospital.' 'Mister, if you want this load of meat, you're from Stony Brook Hospital or else I got troubles from half-a-dozen people around here.' On the spot, I became business manager and assistant treasurer of Stony Brook Hospital!"

Even with such provisions, however, Gilbert Moore recalls too many meals that consisted of beans, beans, and more beans. "I couldn't seem to convince the local ration board that we had a service to perform in feeding these boys at least enough to keep them strong and healthy," he says. "It was a very difficult experience."

Robert S. Swanson, Jr., '43, now a Stony Brook board member, recalls the time his father, president of the S. B. Thomas Baking Company, came out to Stony Brook at his son's request to complain to Dr. Gaebelein about the poor quality of the food. "I'd been telling my father how awful the food was, and he took my word for it. He blasted Dr. Gaebelein for not giving the boys enough good food to eat. Dr. Gaebelein listened to him and then, noting that it was nearly time for dinner, suggested that they go over to the dining room together. When they arrived, my father could catch the odor of the evening meal: it was unmistakably steak! On one of the rare occasions during the whole war, the School had gotten enough coupons together to serve us steak, and that's the day my father chooses to complain about the food! After he finished with me, I never complained about the food again!"

Just as during the Depression, Stony Brook continued granting financial aid during the war years. The school year 1942 to 1943, for example, found Stony Brook committed to aiding boys at a cost of $16,000. When the ledgers were closed, donors had given that sum and $97.88 to spare. Dr. Gaebelein insists that such a consistent record be regarded as evidence of God's blessing upon the School: "Our long-time policy of giving so that others might receive has led to a growing body of contributors. It also means that the principle is true: God will not fail a work which places spiritual aims first.

"The period from the middle of the Depression to the middle of the Second World War was our most difficult so far as student tuition income is concerned. Nevertheless, we never hesitated to continue taking, on faith, the sons of Christian missionaries, pastors, and others who could not afford the tuition. We did this, trusting that the money would be supplied. It has been supplied because God has never failed."

No doubt a secular economist, unfamiliar with the principles of living by an enlightened and responsible faith, would scoff. But the record shows that the principle works. In fact, the record shows that in 1944, Stony Brook had erased its total indebtedness, restored its salaries, and increased its scholarship giving by 50 per cent. Even so, Gaebelein's methods of distributing scholarship aid caused his business manager some consternation. The headmaster's policy was that as long as the School had space available, no qualified candidate would be refused admission because of inability to pay. No fixed ceiling, therefore, was ever put on the scholarship fund. "Frank was and is a man of great faith," Gilbert Moore says, "and he insisted that the blessing of God would always accompany an unselfish Christian benevolence. I agreed, of course, but as the person responsible to the Stony Brook Assembly, Incorporated, for paying the bills, I felt that I ought to know how much the School intended to give away.

"I think, too," Moore goes on to say, "that some boys who received scholarship assistance took it with too little sense of gratitude or lasting indebtedness. In some respects, I'm afraid, Stony Brook was a soft touch. I don't believe our methods of inquiring into a family's ability to pay were as sophisticated as they are today, and I'm sure there were some people who received far more than they truly needed."

One lasting memory still rankles Gilbert Moore's successor, James E. Hill. "We had a boy in school for four years, each year receiving a larger and larger financial grant. Then on graduation day, his father had the nerve to present his son with a smart-looking convertible. And then, to make it worse, he let the kid park the car right in the middle of the campus! I don't know if he intended to say anything to us by this gesture, but I know a lot of people thought so!"

Stony Brook attempted to maintain a healthy attitude during the war. No undue alarm was created over rumors of Nazi submarines in the waters surrounding Long Island. Athletic teams continued to compete successfully, traveling now by railroad and streetcar because of gasoline and tire shortages. But there is no denying that life for some boys was rather grim. The stress of the times did make a difference in the relationships between men and boys.

These were the years when discipline was strict and summary. Dormitory supervision during the evening study period consisted of corridor patrol with frequent room checks to make certain that boys were sitting at their desks in an attitude that suggested attention to duty. Visiting from room to room was forbidden. Consulting with another student on a homework problem was generally frowned upon. To go to the toilet, a boy had to wait at his room door, signal the master on duty, and receive permission. Lights were turned out at an absurdly early hour—10:00 P.M. for seniors—when one considers, first, the fact that assignments demanded more time for thorough completion and, second, the fact that these same young men were supposedly being trained in the responsible use of their time as mature persons.

"What's even more ridiculous," Bob Swanson notes, "is the fact some of our teachers in those years didn't seem to realize that most of us seniors were looking straight down the end of a gun barrel. We knew what our future was. For any of us able to pass the physical, it was the service. In a few months we were going to be soldiers or sailors or flyers. And they treated us like infants!"

Not surprisingly, students found their own means of retaliating against this regimen. The stories of pranks and pranksters out of this period are linked to some of Stony Brook's most notorious hooligans; their victims were some of Stony Brook's most tormented and ineffective teachers. Some of the pranks were intended as innocent fun—hiding alarm clocks set to ring in a classroom or removing the electric fuses for a faculty apartment. Other so-called pranks carried deeper connotations of ill will toward particular men—dropping bags of water upon a faculty wife or leaving the carcass of a mangled rabbit or squirrel at an apartment door.

The petty offender was punished by the loss of privileges and perhaps by being assigned to the coal piles behind each major building. There he shoveled coal into the bin through a basement window until his sins had been atoned. The serious offender was dispatched—perhaps suspended for a couple of weeks or separated outrightly from the School.

Some of the mischief may have resulted from Stony Brook's narrow policy regarding boys and girls. Isolated in a tiny Long Island village, boys at Stony Brook did not find many eligible young ladies in the community; those few who did were certain that their romances were closely watched. Back issues of school newspapers and literary journals carry very little news of parties or socials to which girls were invited. When they were, Stony Brook's unwritten-but-understood taboo against dancing imposed an added restriction. Nevertheless, there were various other forms of entertainment offered. Occasionally, Stony Brook's most distinguished alumnus-musician, pianist Jorge Bolet, '34, would give a recital, returning to Stony Brook sometimes to play duo piano works with Dr. Gaebelein.

The taboo against dancing interfered with those who wished to "swing and sway with Sammy Kaye." Instead, they groaned, at Stony Brook you "sit and sweat with Jorge Bolet." Still the Stony Brook sophisticates kept in touch with show business through radio and recordings. The big bands of the Dorsey brothers, Harry James,

Glen Gray, and others were especially popular, and schoolboy columnists in *The Blue and White* kept their readers informed about which "Beat-Me-Daddy-Eight-to-the-Bar" recording was worth purchasing, which trumpet virtuoso had been drafted, which drummer had switched bands and why. Some daring aficionados would even sneak in to New York's·famous Paramount Theater to hear Frank Sinatra.

Saturday night brought a variety of lectures, travelogues, recent newsreel films about the war, magicians, fly-casting experts, and other one-night-stand performers, including a little known actor who was just developing a characterization of Mark Twain, the now-famous Hal Holbrook.

* * *

During World War II, Stony Brook sent 472 men into service, of whom 22 gave their lives. As the School neared its twenty-fifth year, Dr. Gaebelein began to think of a major memorial to these alumni, similar to the long-delayed Carson Hall. He urged the board repeatedly to take initiative toward the fulfillment of this goal. Certainly the board had every reason to share his optimism. The estate of the late Dr. W. McLean Yost of Baltimore, Maryland had bequeathed the School its largest gift to date, properties valued at more than $200,000. With only token solicitation toward a Twenty-Fifth Anniversary Fund, more than $43,000 had been raised in 1946. More could be expected as designated gifts for a library in memory of Dr. Arno C. Gaebelein, who had recently died.

Yet there seemed to be a sluggishness toward the project within the board of trustees. Well into 1947, the Silver Anniversary Year, plans were still uncertain, committees stalemated, and leadership lacking. Frank Gaebelein does not often allow his anger to show through his writing, but in his 1947 report to the board, he spoke his mind:

> Too long has our teaching been carried on in over-crowded, unattractive, and ill-ventilated classrooms. Too long have our library facilities been inadequate. With a faculty and student body such as ours, Stony Brook has a right to classrooms which at least compare with those in a small town high school. Our Chapel, gymnasium, and infirmary are first-class. Our classrooms and library are perhaps third-class. Yet Stony Brook is first and foremost a school.

He went on to tell the board that the proposed Memorial Hall was "far more than a desirable addition to our resources" and could no longer be postponed indefinitely. Then Gaebelein turned on all the moral pressure he could exert—arguments from historical comparison, from present claims to spirituality, and from responsible stewardship:

> Many years ago at Northfield, the late Dr. Henry Clay Trumbull made an address with the title, "The Duty of Making the Past a Success." Such a duty faces this Board during this Silver Anniversary Year.

But even this appeal failed, and the twenty-fifth anniversary came and went, in 1947, with little more than an alumni brochure to mark the occasion. The brochure contained many gratifying commendations from the presidents of New York University, Columbia University, Lafayette College, and others as well as distinguished civic leaders and prominent pastors. But the board had slackened in its commitment, and the needed buildings had not been built.

Frank Gaebelein knows the value of tradition and the importance of maintaining ties with the honored past. He also knows that most people, even generous people, need an occasion on which to give. Twice he had seen the possibility of using a landmark occasion to honor John F. Carson's memory slip away—once, as he has said, in the providence of God just prior to the Depression. But this second failure he found harder to accept as the action of God's providence; it seemed more like the inaction of men's will.

By 1949, a new mood seems to have entered into Gaebelein's relationship with the board. He was no longer the novice headmaster; he had proved himself and his School. Although some trustees were less interested in progress, he was looking ahead. It was time for a change. Hugh R. Monro, a wise businessman who had served as president of the board since the death of Dr. Carson in 1927, retired and was succeeded by Judge A. Marshall Thompson of Pittsburgh, Pennsylvania.

Together with Judge Thompson, Frank Gaebelein revised his building objective from the larger structure to a schoolhouse that would satisfy the absolutely minimum needs of a growing school. This building would contain classrooms, laboratories, offices, and a library wing. Dedicated in April 1951, the building called Memorial

Hall had cost only $175,000 and was occupied free of debt. According to the scale of rising construction costs, the same building delayed by only a year might have cost twice the amount. Indeed, a wing of only four additional classrooms, built in 1957, cost nearly as much as the original structure.

Why did Stony Brook fail to achieve what it needed and might have had? One can look for answers in the postwar economy and, remembering the sudden rush toward a new materialism after the restrictions of wartime rationing had been lifted, blame the failure on a lack of support by Christian people. Certainly it is true that most Americans were more concerned about replacing a worn sofa and the rattling prewar automobile than they were about making contributions to any school. But all such reasoning evades a central issue. Stony Brook's governing board had grown weary in welldoing.

Some members, by their repeated absences from trustee meetings, had reduced themselves to names on a letterhead. The Stony Brook School was simply not their major interest. Others lacked the ability to create and maintain the kind of momentum a school must have from its leadership if it is to make progress. Among the exceptions to this condemnation were Dr. A. Gordon MacLennan, a Scottish Presbyterian of strength and conviction whose support of the School never flagged, and Dr. Donald Grey Barnhouse, the radio Bible teacher, pastor, and editor of *Eternity* magazine whose wide ministry often benefited Stony Brook. In fact, the young pastor who now preaches from Barnhouse's pulpit at Tenth Presbyterian Church in Philadelphia, Dr. James M. Boice, '56, came to Stony Brook as a result of Dr. Barnhouse's encouragement.

Still other board members, however, could not reconcile themselves to the clear fact that the School, although still under the sponsorship of the Stony Brook Assembly, had moved out from under that parental wing to take on an identity of its own.

In some respects, the crisis over the construction of Memorial Hall signaled the beginning of the end for the Stony Brook Assembly and its summer conference program. Frank Gaebelein had made his position clear: "Stony Brook is first and foremost a school." Some trustees strongly disagreed. Nowhere is their policy more clearly demonstrated than in the matter of faculty housing during the summer months.

From the first summer following a school year, the summer of 1923, until the Assembly discontinued its conferences in 1957, faculty families were expected to relinquish their apartments in the dormitories to house conference guests. Teachers were given the option of finding accommodations elsewhere or accepting much smaller quarters in what now became a summer conference hotel. Fortunately, most faculty had summer plans that took them to jobs in a boarding camp or to graduate study. But even for them there was the annual reshuffling of their personal belongings—clothing and furniture—to a loft above the auditorium and back again at summer's end. Their apartments were converted into rented rooms.

This summer shakeup became so burdensome after a few years that several teachers chose not to continue at Stony Brook rather than face the annual disruption in housing. Their leaving was a loss which Stony Brook could have avoided by a more enlightened policy on the part of the board toward its faculty.

Frank Gaebelein contested this policy unsuccessfully. The board felt its faculty should be willing to sustain this hardship for the good of the whole enterprise. He was aided finally by some young couples who refused to accept such Byzantine treatment and threatened squatters' rights. By asserting themselves to the headmaster, they raised the status of the Stony Brook teacher to a level above that of an Assembly employee. The fact that Stony Brook was able to keep as many faculty content to remain year after year is a quiet tribute to Dr. Gaebelein's persuasiveness, as well as the loyalty of those men and women.

"The problems of housing in a boarding school are endless," Frank Gaebelein says. "In my experience they were often among the most trying difficulties I faced. Where to put a man so that he and his family would be comfortable, so that each dormitory would be adequately maintained, so that I could be fair to some sense of seniority, yet so that I wasn't tied to any rigid system of promotion through housing—these were the year-by-year problems to solve."

These problems still exist, and Donn Gaebelein, like his father before him, must make the annual decisions as to who lives where. Stony Brook has eleven apartments for faculty in its dormitories. These quarters range from two rooms with kitchenette and bath to six rooms. Four of these apartments are duplex. On the fringe of the campus stand twelve houses owned by the School; six of these have been built since 1970. Other houses are owned by teachers, while the School rents two houses just off-campus.

Routinely a young man accepting a position at Stony Brook must expect to live in a dormitory for several years—six to eight, on the average—until a school-owned house opens through resignation or retirement. Occasionally, an older man will be appointed to receive private housing from the beginning because of his experience.

In the past some dormitory-bound teachers, looking ahead and unable to see any likelihood of school houses becoming available, have set out on their own to purchase houses adjacent to the campus. But such housing is now extremely expensive and taxes are soaring; therefore, the School has begun a program of housing construction, with houses ringing the campus and serving as a natural hedge for the property.

When the Stony Brook Assembly founded its school for boys in 1922, neither Dr. Carson nor his associates could foresee a time when the School would engulf the then-flourishing summer conferences. The School was clearly an auxiliary to the principal work of the Assembly. In spite of the fact that the School occupied the grounds for three-quarters of the year, the six or eight weeks of summer activities were considered primary for several reasons. Numbers, for example: in a single conference week far more people attended the meetings of the Assembly than were enrolled in the School. Multiplied over the span of the entire conference schedule, the summer influence of Stony Brook far exceeded the school-term influence.

Stony Brook's summer clientele was mostly adult, although youth conferences were held. The goodwill engendered toward the Stony Brook Assembly among Christian adults might very well carry over in contributions both to the conferences and to the School. Certainly this was true of many donors, whose only connection with Stony Brook had been as a conference guest.

Gilbert Moore casts some further light of his own on the intricate corporate structure of the Stony Brook Assembly. "The original deed of trust," he says, "established the Assembly as an eleemosynary institution sponsoring religious conferences. As an extension of that primary work, there would also be a school. In fact, I recall a suggestion that, in addition to the school for boys, there also be a school for girls located in Belle Terre, near Port

Jefferson. All this, of course, was long before I came to work for the Assembly in 1929. But by that time, it was becoming clear to some of the old-timers on the Assembly board that the tail was beginning to wag the dog. The Stony Brook School was beginning to dominate the affairs of the Assembly.

"The Assembly was the parent body, and in the minds of some of these men, that's the way it had always been and that's the way it would stay."

The Stony Brook Assembly, of course, owned all the property holdings used by the School, as well as some property not used by the School. For example, one of Long Island's finest restaurants, the Three Village Inn, located between the Stony Brook village green and the water front, was once a hotel for Assembly guests. Nearby stood a few harbor-view cottages, and above them on Knolltop Hill, a ramshackle meeting hall where some of the Assembly's services convened for the benefit of those guests who were not accommodated on the main campus. When the Assembly consolidated all its activities on the campus and no longer needed the village properties, they were sold and the funds credited to the Assembly's account.

Yet at the very time of this sale, the School was passing through some of its bleakest days. The budget for the School was running at $80,000 annually; the conferences had an income of $3000 and expenses of $4000—about 5 per cent as great as the School. Still the Stony Brook Assembly regarded itself as the parent organization and its primary work was the conference ministry. "The money from the sale of those village properties," says Gilbert Moore, "went toward summer expenses."

In retrospect, a single detail tells a great deal about the respect of the Stony Brook board for its school during those years. A complete set of the minutes shows no record of a board meeting at Stony Brook during the school term, until 1952. While school was in session, the board met at the National Republican Club or at the New York State Chamber of Commerce Building or in the private offices of a trustee; never, apparently, on the campus of the School. Annually, however, the board met *on the conference grounds* usually in late August during the well-attended General Bible Conference.

More and more the leadership of the Stony Brook Assembly

began to turn toward laymen—attorneys, bankers, and other businessmen—although the remaining clergymen were almost always Presbyterians. But if Presbyterian strength brought spiritual vigor to the Stony Brook program, it also meant, as far as Gilbert Moore was concerned, that there was an overbalance of clergymen and sometimes a spirit of rancor.

"Through most of the years I worked with the Stony Brook Assembly," he says, "I felt that the board consisted of too many ministers and too few men of business acumen. And so far as the laymen were concerned, most of them were also committed, somewhat more or less, to other Christian enterprises. Hugh Monro, for example, had responsibilities to the American Tract Society. It was often hard for those of us who were on the job at Stony Brook— Frank Gaebelein, Pierson Curtis, and me—to get a sense of real loyalty to Stony Brook."

An affinity between Presbyterians and Stony Brook maintained the historic fact that John F. Carson had himself been a Presbyterian minister and moderator of the General Assembly. But there was an even tighter bond, a legal obligation to the Boards of Foreign and National Missions of the Presbyterian Church, U.S.A. The document incorporating the Stony Brook Assembly, filed with the County Clerk on May 18, 1914, contained the following conditional limitation:

> That in the event the said premises shall cease to be used for the purpose set forth . . . , the said party of the second part [the Stony Brook Assembly] shall grant and convey the said premises in fee simple, unconditionally, to the Boards of Home and Foreign Missions of the Presbyterian Church, U.S.A., share and share alike.

"The purpose set forth," of course, was the originating purpose of establishing a center for religious and educational activities based upon the Platform of Principles. It is a curious irony of history that the founders of the Stony Brook Assembly should have felt secure in binding their enterprise to the theological steadfastness of the Presbyterian Church, U.S.A. and its missionary boards as warders against future apostasy. The founders were sure that, if after their deaths those then responsible for the Stony Brook Assembly should forsake its Principles, the Presbyterian boards would take over and preserve Stony Brook's integrity. The ensuing decades have shown, however, that the official theological direction of the Presbyterian Church, U.S.A. has been increasingly awry from the trust John F. Carson, Ford C. Ottman, Maitland Alexander, and others committed to their denomination.

As early as 1945, Dr. Roy M. Hart, a Brooklyn lawyer and treasurer of the Assembly, recommended that the Assembly endeavor to have this reverter clause removed "through securing quit claim deeds from the Boards in question," as the minutes record. The legal proceedings, begun in 1964, were not completed until 1970 when The Stony Brook School, Incorporated stood free of all external entanglements, including the dissolved Stony Brook Assembly. The School also obtained, through the generosity of the current boards, its release from the Board of Home Missions, the Board of National Missions, and the Commission on Ecumenical Mission and Relations of the United Presbyterian Church, U.S.A., successors to the orginal holders of the reversion deed.

5

The Ongoing Experiment

In the period following World War II, no decision has had more sweeping effect than the 1954 Supreme Court decision in the case of *Brown v. Board of Education*, ruling against racial segregation in public schools. The history of that decision has been recounted elsewhere in detail. Here it is enough to note that until the 1954 decision, the law of the land had been interpreted in light of the precedent established by *Plessy v. Ferguson,* an 1896 Supreme Court judgment in favor of "separate but equal" facilities.

For most of evangelical Christianity, this social situation presented no moral problem at all. In some Christian circles, the black man was treated as the object of a divine curse upon the sons of Ham. In others, he was treated as an object for overseas evangelization—a naked pagan in missionary films from David Livingstone's *Dark Continent.* In more benign churches, the black man's music was sung with hardly any awareness of the irony in a white choir's singing "Let My People Go."

The American independent school reflected the unconcern of American society at large. While denying any inferences of outright bigotry, most administrators would say, "We'd be glad to have a black student if we knew any who were qualified and who could make the adjustment to boarding school life." Although these same headmasters had no difficulty in finding and sponsoring impoverished white boys, as well as some Orientals, Latin Americans, or a rare Nigerian, there seemed to be a shortage of available American Negroes.

Stony Brook was no different from other independent schools in this respect. In the early 1940s, Frank Gaebelein had discussed the admission of black students with the board of trustees; the matter had been set aside. In 1948, he wrote to Hugh R. Monro, the board president, "I do not think we can meet the issue by ignoring it." But again the problem was tabled, indicative of the board's reluctance. There were no concrete expressions of bigotry, just an eloquent absence of black students. If questioned about its attitude toward an interracial student body, the School could always point to its several Oriental students.

Finally, in 1955, Stony Brook admitted its first American black, Laurence Foster, Jr. Dr. Gaebelein's announcement to the trustees must be understood in the context of its times; otherwise, it appears to be unnecessarily apologetic:

> The board should know that the present student body includes an American Negro student. The son of a professor of sociology at Lincoln Memorial University, Oxford, Pennsylvania, he is making a good adjustment to Stony Brook. We have not heard the slightest objection to his presence in school from any source—boys, faculty, or parents.

Foster's recollections of his experience at Stony Brook reveal the stress of his mixed reception. He says, "Stony Brook was for me a fairly worthwhile experience. I was integrated with little apparent difficulty."

In each of the next few years, one or two black students enrolled at Stony Brook. They were almost uniformly the sons of professional people—doctors, teachers, musicians, or military officers— accustomed to moving with poise between the black and white sectors of society. If their relationship with faculty and students was polite, it was also mutually overcautious, as if neither blacks nor whites were sure of the protocol of human relations.

This was the period of testing for all of Stony Brook's previous claims. Could the School, which rested its very reason for being upon the truth of God's Word, fail to acknowledge that "God is no respector of persons?" Could the School, which sang,

> *In Christ there is no East or West,*
> *In Him no South or North;*
> *But one great fellowship of love*
> *Throughout the whole wide earth,*

exclude some from that fellowship because of race?

The obvious answer had already been given, but it was not enough to remain passive, waiting for black families of some means to approach the School. In 1962, Dr. Gaebelein's final year as headmaster, he began to solicit the help of various agencies in finding black candidates. The Boys' Club of New York City was such an agency working with disadvantaged blacks and Puerto Ricans, providing an initial screening and selection from which the School could draw.

Soon, however, Stony Brook discovered that through the normal channels of its connection with various urban pastors it could make its own decisions, backed by the support of a neighborhood church. One such church is the Elmendorf Reformed Church in East Harlem, where the Reverend Don DeYoung is the pastor. This is also the church with which the School co-operates in sponsoring a one-week summer camp in the Catskill Mountains.

"I've never doubted or regretted the decision we made to open Stony Brook to all races," says Frank Gaebelein. "How could we have done otherwise and maintain a position of Christian integrity? Of course, one always wishes that the decision had been made sooner. But one must operate with the light given. It's not what we neglect to do out of ignorance that condemns us; it's what we neglect to do when we know to do better.

"Stony Brook is in the fore among Christian schools in the matter of providing an education for black students. This is, clearly, a testimony to the practical Christianity we have always upheld. The Scriptures say that 'Jesus went about doing good.' So must we."

Frank Gaebelein views a school like Stony Brook as a microcosm of society at large, not an isolated colony removed from the rest of the world. "A school like Stony Brook should be a community in which one finds the experiences of the larger world beyond," he says. For this reason, Stony Brook has never believed in a philosophy of learning-in-order-to-live, as though learning and living were not simultaneous experiences. Charles Silberman speaks of young people's need "to break out of the constraints that keep them disengaged" from society's problems. Thus, he says, the schools must "make these years rewarding in their own right, and not merely a preparation for the next stage of life." Accordingly, the School encourages each person's acquaintance with the richness of his own life and culture as well as with the culture of other persons with whom he must share his adult world. The emphasis, more properly, falls upon living-in-order-to-learn.

Some partisans of the American public school, such as William

H. Kilpatrick and James B. Conant, have tried to argue that private education is "disunifying" to the American republic. Kilpatrick, for instance, wrote: "Private and parochial schools isolate their students from democratic society and accordingly create national inconsistency and disunity." President Conant repeated the fallacy in his book, *Education and Liberty:*

> The greater the proportion of our youth who fail to attend our public schools and who receive their education elsewhere, the greater threat to our democratic unity.

At Stony Brook, as at many other boarding schools, the converse is true. A room housing three boys in Monro Hall, for instance, finds the son of a metropolitan bank executive, a missionary's son from Central America, and a black from Bedford-Stuyvesant. Such a mix is rarely found in the typical American high school, drawing as it does from its immediate locale. Far from being an anomaly to American democracy, a school with Stony Brook's mixed population becomes a close approximation to the real circumstances within the nation.

* * *

In his last years at Stony Brook, Frank Gaebelein withstood strong pressures from the fundamentalist wing of evangelical Christianity. The founders of the Stony Brook Assembly, though Presbyterian in the majority, had been from various denominations and had held differing views on some matters of doctrine. But they had satisfied their need for unanimity in the Platform of Principles. If a man could affirm his belief in these articles, it did not matter whether his theology were labeled "pre-tribulational" or "amillenial."

But over the years since the Fundamentalist-Modernist schism of the twenties, some of the more contentious fundamentalists took issue with what they considered to be a dangerous trend toward liberalism at Stony Brook. They did not hesitate to create a hierarchy of values by which Christian schools should be judged and thereafter supported. The most important of these values, after compulsory daily chapel services and Bible study—both of which Stony Brook maintained—were the negative standards by which these particular Christians measured the faith of others: personal prohibitions against smoking, drinking, theater going, dancing, and card playing. Along with these taboos loomed their condemnation for compromise of any sort with "the ecumenical movement." Among these narrower sects of Christianity, sharing the pulpit with anyone whose theological pedigree may be doubtful, is tantamount, in fundamentalist categories, to blasphemy.

Stony Brook has always stood up against this kind of pressure, whether it expressed itself in terms of ecclesiastical affiliation, conformity in its curriculum, doctrinal bias, or personal standards of behavior. In the 1930s, for example, when theological wars were dividing the Presbyterian denomination in the North, Stony Brook welcomed both Dr. J. Ross Stevenson, president of Princeton Theological Seminary, and Dr. J. Gresham Machen of the dissenting Westminster Theological Seminary. When the effect of the Scopes trial of 1925 made any passing reference to evolution a cardinal sin, Frank Gaebelein did not interrogate his science teachers or make an issue of Darwin's theory. "I let my Christian teachers teach," he says. "I trusted them as teachers just as I trusted them in other capacities. We didn't ignore evolution as a hypothesis in the history of ideas; we just didn't allow it as dogma."

The same is true of patented interpretations of the Bible. The name Gaebelein is associated with biblical prophecy and with the old Scofield Reference Bible. In its original edition, the Scofield Bible had taken a strong position in favor of *dispensationalism,* the view that God has divided human history into periods other than *before* and *after* Christ and that during these periods his work has been with different peoples and by different means. Arno C. Gaebelein was a famous prophetic preacher; he had served on the committee of the original Scofield Reference Bible, and his son served on subsequent committees. But the influence of the elder Gaebelein was never passed on in any dogmatic manner to the faculty of The Stony Brook School. *Dispensationalism* as such never became a necessary tenet of faith; nor has any other limiting view, for as St. Peter said, "No prophecy of the scripture is of any private interpretation."

The same attitudes held true with regard to standards of personal conduct. Stony Brook had its strict code of behavior, which on the surface appeared little different from the index of fundamentalist taboos. But closer inspection revealed that smoking, for example, at

Stony Brook was not forbidden because it was officially considered
sinful—although some faculty would have believed so—but because
of known fire hazards and the suspected detriment to health.
Likewise card playing was not treated as evil in itself—several
faculty couples met for bridge parties—but the urge to gamble with
cards was considered potentially demoralizing to a closely tied
community. Drinking simply had no place in a boys' school, but Dr.
Gaebelein's annual sermon on abstinence stressed the idea of
personal character against mindless conformity more than it argued
against alcoholic beverages. Boys whose parents permitted them to
were free to attend movies, and the School encouraged attendance
at New York performances of theater, opera, and ballet. Regarding
social dancing, Gaebelein's attitude was ambivalent although the
trustees were fixed. He deplored the fact that so many young people
could find so little to say to each other at a party that they depended
upon dancing for a substitute. But he also conceded that there are
far greater pitfalls in life than dancing, now permitted and closely
supervised at school parties.

Most of all, Frank Gaebelein opposed those who wished the
Christian school to become a haven in which young people might
hide from the world. Some observers mistakenly regarded Stony
Brook as a glorified Sunday School from which angelic adolescents
were stamped out as missionaries or preachers. Gaebelein shud-
dered to hear that an administrator of another Christian school had
assured parents at commencement exercises, "Your sons and
daughters have had a safe education."

"These terms must always remain mutually exclusive," Dr.
Gaebelein declares. "No matter how well-meant, such expressions
are reactionary, basically anti-intellectual, and patently un-
Christian. Why, the essence of a sound liberal education is its power
to unshackle the mind from the ignorance that binds it. A Christian
liberal education frees the mind from all that is untrue, including
some of the legalistic taboos adopted by some Christians.

"The difficulty," Dr. Gaebelein goes on, "is that too many
Christian people aren't aware of the purpose of a fine preparatory
school. Too often such parents think of a school like Stony Brook
and others as a last resort in straightening out a difficult child. They
don't realize that our primary function is to educate young men and
women of superior ability and sound character. After all, our chief

aim is training for Christian leadership. A school can't achieve that aim by hedging its students against the realities of life beyond the campus."

This tendency among some schools to protect rather than prepare its students has led the Yale University chaplain, William Sloane Coffin, Jr., to accuse "the small Christian schools out there in the middle of no place" of being "so concerned with preserving students from urban vices that we don't give them a chance to develop some virtue by being involved with urban problems. That is why small Christian schools turn out small Christians."

Facing the retrenchment of fundamentalism, Frank Gaebelein was affirming his agreement with the principles of "the new evangelicalism" of Harold John Ockenga and others. Dr. Ockenga, for many years pastor of the Park Street Church in Boston, president of Fuller Theological Seminary, and now president of Gordon College and Gordon-Conwell Divinity School, had created the term, "the new evangelicalism" to describe both "an adherence to orthodoxy and an interest in the sociological problems of the day." Both at Fuller Seminary and from his historic pulpit, Dr. Ockenga had declared the need for a new awakening among Christians to contemporary social problems.

With this commitment Frank Gaebelein agreed. Stony Brook would retain its foundational view of the Bible's importance to Christian experience. But Stony Brook would continue to avoid the negative standards of fundamentalism, the isolationism of parochial Christianity as practiced by some of Stony Brook's constituents. Perhaps Dr. Gaebelein's most open break with narrow Christianity came in 1957, when he joined the Executive Committee for the Billy Graham Crusade in Madison Square Garden. In his capacity as a committeeman, Gaebelein worked closely with Christians from every sector of the Church, much to the dismay of some not so ecumenically minded. When one of the post-crusade regional rallies was held on the Stony Brook campus, with some six thousand persons attending, criticism heightened to a fury. Moreover, the decision of the Stony Brook Assembly to discontinue its residential summer conferences that same summer seemed to coincide with an apparent slide toward apostasy.

Criticism of Frank Gaebelein personally and of the School indirectly came from many quarters, sometimes in letters of scathing rebuke. Other correspondents were deeply puzzled. One woman from Indiana, whose pastor had chosen to make a sweeping indictment of Billy Graham and all who were his active supporters, wrote to ask: How could Gaebelein co-operate with Graham who co-operated with persons whose theology was questionable? Dr. Gaebelein replied:

> I am distressed at the attitude of the critics of Billy Graham and his work. To be very definite, it almost seems that many of these critics would prefer to have the hundreds and thousands of people who have been truly saved in the Crusades lost than to have them saved in meetings, all the arrangements for which they cannot approve. I should prefer to stand with God who has been leading people to Christ through the devoted ministry of Billy Graham and his associates.

* * *

During these same concluding years of his administration, Frank Gaebelein endeavored to make Stony Brook more than just a leading *Christian* school. His intention was to regain the early recognition for excellence that had suffered through financial adversity. In the mid-fifties he began a systematic upgrading of faculty standards. For many years he had operated on the principle that the right man could be molded into an adequate teacher. Stony Brook had known more than its share of fine men who were merely adequate teachers. Dr. Gaebelein now raised his sights to look for men who were indeed *masters* (the preparatory school term for *teachers*) of their subjects.

The board of trustees responded to his insistence that faculty salaries be brought into competitive range with other independent schools. He was particularly concerned for his younger faculty, those living in dormitory apartments and receiving meals for their families in the School's dining room. In 1960, for example, the average Stony Brook teacher in this category was 28 years old and had two children. His cash salary was less than $3500. This was one thousand dollars less than the next lowest average salary paid by thirty-two independent schools in the northeastern United States. (By 1972, the average age and family size remains about the same; happily, the salary scale has risen to just above the median figures for boarding schools published by the National Association of Independent Schools.)

Frank Gaebelein was conscious of the need to improve working conditions in other areas as well: better living accommodations and a fairer distribution of responsibilities, more voice in administrative policy making, and assistance for graduate study. These policies made it possible, by the time of his retirement in 1963, for Gaebelein to present a faculty of twenty men and two women generally more proficient in their fields of specialization than previously had been the case.

Tighter entrance requirements requiring standardized testing and an interview at Stony Brook for most candidates also raised the academic tone of the School. The College Entrance Examination Board's advanced placement examinations were being offered so that qualified students could obtain college credit for their studies at Stony Brook. Homogeneous grouping of students in English, mathematics, and foreign languages was now possible because of a larger faculty. With 211 students from 18 states and 15 other countries, Stony Brook had a ratio, in 1963, of better than one instructor to every ten boys.

But Gaebelein knew that not enough had been done academically to meet the needs of every graduate. One wrote, in 1962, out of his experience at Stony Brook in the late fifties:

> I have found on looking back, that when I left Stony Brook I had little of what might be called intellectual curiosity, a hunger for knowledge.

This was a stinging blow to a man, himself a scholar, who wanted his students to mature in an environment conducive to Christian scholarship. Sensing that the spirit of the alumnus was constructive, Gaebelein began his lengthy reply by acknowledging the validity of much of the young man's criticism. But, he went on to point out:

> I feel that some of the points you make are more applicable to the school as you knew it than to Stony Brook today. After all, schools change and progress. Even in the four or five years since you were here, there has been a marked forward movement at Stony Brook intellectually.

The present senior class, Dr. Gaebelein told him, consisted of forty boys, four of whom were National Merit Scholarship finalists. These four were all authentic Stony Brook products, having entered the school in the eighth, ninth, or tenth grades. "A school that does not allow scope for independent thought," Gaebelein contended, "would not be able to challenge and hold the interest of boys of this caliber." The Stony Brook Class of 1958, just completing college, had enrolled at some thirty different colleges and universities, including each of the Ivy League colleges, as well as other highly selective colleges such as Colgate, Duke, Union College, and Washington and Lee. Surely some of these facts, he argued, suggested academic changes for the better at Stony Brook.

The School was also taking a great deal more care in the matter of college placement. The times of stress in college admissions had begun, and with changes in college admissions officers and policies a school no longer could merely send its transcripts and recommendations and expect its student to be accepted. Marvin W. Goldberg, director of studies and college placement counselor since 1945, was now beginning to counsel boys early in the junior year about the selection of a college.

Stony Brook's concern for the boy's choice of college was one of the features about the School that impressed the *New York Herald Tribune* columnist, Al Laney, who reported on his one-day visit to Stony Brook:

> It is unlikely there is anywhere a school which better serves its boys in the matter of helping them select a college best suited to their needs and their desires. There is a deep and genuine concern here over this matter and a great deal of thought and prayer goes into it.

Then Laney remarked that among the private schools he had visited some seemed more concerned over what a boy's choice of college can mean for the school rather than for the boy himself.

> Not at Stony Brook, though. Here they are not at all concerned that great numbers of their boys make it into Harvard, Yale, and Princeton, the Ivy colleges or even the Eastern colleges. Their concern is that the boy find the right college, no matter where, and in this they certainly are making a contribution to American education, as they assert. For this is a thing in which some of our most famous boys schools are woefully remiss.

But though Stony Brook was deserving of acclaim for its program of college counseling and placement, certain pronounced weaknesses in the curriculum kept the School from the right to claims of excellence. Some of the weaknesses could be attributed to inadequate facilities—the science department, ever since Clyde Mellinger first set up his laboratory in Hopkins Hall basement, had never had the kind of space and equipment found in most run-of-the-mill high schools. Other soft spots in the curriculum might be blamed on the relatively small size of enrollment and faculty: With only so many persons, only so many courses may be offered effectively.

The most apparent weakness, however, and the most ironic, was in the fine arts. The School that had begun with a conservatory graduate offering instruction in music to almost all the students did not have a qualified, resident music instructor except for a brief interim when the baritone Frank Boggs came to teach. The School whose neighbor and patron was the distinguished American painter, Paul King, conducted its art instruction as a Friday evening club activity. Unless a particularly spunky group of students persevered to bring off a production, the only function of the Drama Club in most years was to meet for its annual yearbook photograph.

It is not fair to characterize Stony Brook as a cultural wasteland during all these years. Even in the lean period of the Depression, when there was little enough money for the absolute essentials, there were still evidences of an active cultural awareness. A school newspaper, professionally printed, appeared every two weeks and with a quality of writing that exceeds anything produced by Stony Brookers today. The Radio Club met weekly to listen to "The Voice of Firestone" and other similar programs. Another group listened to the Metropolitan Opera broadcasts. Boys were entertained in the headmaster's home, and some learned there to appreciate the literature of the piano.

Still, these experiences with the arts of writing and music, painting, and drama were without sequence and planning. They *happened* because this master or that boy was enthusiastic enough to persist in his interest and by his persistence influenced others.

When questioned about this lack, Frank Gaebelein acknowledges the defect in Stony Brook's concern for the arts during his administration. "I'm pleased to see so much activity in music and drama at Stony Brook today, but the problem I faced was always one of a shortage of money and the unhappy decision in favor of higher priorities. When I had only a certain amount to spend and I needed, say, either a mathematics teacher or someone qualified to teach music or art, I had to make my decision for mathematics."

Dr. Gaebelein's solution was to hire persons with a secondary interest in the arts or part-time teachers from the community; then, to augment their work, he brought fine musicians and some artists to the campus. "I have always felt," he says, "that the actual performance or presentation of excellent art is a superior model to a mundane course in music appreciation or art history." This argument assumes, of course, that the classroom study of music or the history of art will be dull. In theory Stony Brook managed to eke out a cultural program through its chapel choir and glee club, the few boys who studied piano privately, and the visits of guest musicians or of art exhibitions. But it is certainly true that the bulk of Stony Brook's graduates over almost four decades received less than a smattering acquaintance with the great music and art the headmaster himself knew and appreciated.

Perhaps Gaebelein thought that the mass exposure of an audience of restless boys to a piano recital would kindle in some an appreciation like his own. He certainly believed this to be true of school-wide singing. For many years the choir director, whoever he happened to be, had taken a weekly chapel service for group singing. After his visits to English schools during 1952-53, his sabbatical year, Dr. Gaebelein became convinced that the full-harmony singing he had heard could be reproduced in Hegeman Memorial Chapel also. He prevailed upon his virtually untrained choir director to try, with the result that what passed for choral singing was accomplished *en masse*. Dr. Gaebelein was sufficiently satisfied, however, to comment on the experience in *Christianity Today:*

> Each year the whole school of 200 plus the faculty is organized for part singing. Through weekly rehearsals, we learn some great music and sing it at public occasions such as the annual academic convocation [the Initiation Ritual for The *Cum Laude* Society] or the baccalaureate service. Thus we have learned choruses from *The Messiah,* a *Gloria* from one of Mozart's Masses, some Bach, and this year we are working on a chorus from Haydn's *Creation.* It is refreshing to hear adolescent boys humming or singing Mozart or Handel as they walk about the campus. . . . But one speaks of these things with humility, realizing how much more should be done.

Much more is being done in the arts today at Stony Brook. Students may obtain instruction and performance experience in vocal and instrumental music from skilled teachers; music history and theory are taught. Dramatic productions are staged throughout the year with students learning each aspect of the theatrical arts— from designing sets to directing plays. Studio art remains an elective working out of makeshift quarters, but each year seems to reveal a new group of painters and sculptors.

At least it may now be said that Stony Brook regards the artist as highly as the athlete. This was not always so. The School had always given a high priority to sports, and the traditions begun in the Mellinger era—with solid football and basketball victories over much larger high schools all over Long Island—had continued into the 1960s, particularly in wrestling and in track. In these sports, Stony Brook dominated the Ivy Preparatory School League. Marvin Goldberg's cross-country teams were looking for college freshmen to compete against. His prize runner, Robin Lingle, '60, had set a new standard for schoolboy endurance when, in 1959, he won two cross-country championship races on the same day. In the morning, he won the Eastern States' title, defeating stellar runners from New England to Washington, D. C. Just three hours later he returned to the Van Cortlandt Park starting line for another two-and-one-half-mile race, this time for the Ivy League victory. *The New York Times* applauded Lingle's remarkable achievement.

To some at Stony Brook, it seemed that athletics held a place second only to the activities at Hegeman Memorial Chapel. The debating team met at six o'clock in the morning to accommodate four of its members whose varsity athletic commitments involved daily afternoon practices. On the occasion of the Ivy League debate tournament, Stony Brook's best affirmative debater, a reserve baseball player, could not accompany the debate team because he was needed to sit on the baseball bench. Not long thereafter debating as an interschool activity died at Stony Brook.

One wonders whether Dr. Gaebelein was aware of those conditions. Surely he realized that other aspects of a boy's whole learning experience were suffering from an overdose of athleticism. So, too, were some members of his faculty. Like many independent schools, Stony Brook prided itself on having a versatile faculty— scholars in the classroom and coaches on the field. Certainly, Stony Brook had a goodly number of coaches with collegiate experience in the sport to which they were assigned. But there were always the junior varsity and freshman teams, not to mention the intramural exercise program for the "sick, lame, and lazy," which must also be covered. To fill these assignments, almost every man was needed to take a season's turn, no matter how ill-disposed he felt toward athletics. The results were sometimes discouraging, often disorganized, and tended toward outright poor discipline in athletics. One young teacher assigned to coach freshman baseball offered as his standard workout: "Okay, all you guys get out there, and I'll try to hit it over your head!"

To justify the ten hours and more each week that boys spent in varsity sports—the man-hours spent by faculty coaches would have been astounding, had they ever been calculated—Stony Brook's athletic director, Floyd Johnson, once wrote in the School's quarterly bulletin:

> The athletic program is an important part in the life of a prep school student, especially if it is coordinated with interscholastic activities. It can develop school spirit and promote loyalty and pride for the school. It can also be one of the unifying factors of the student body. A good athletic program is a great morale builder, as well as a relaxer.

Unquestionably, there were important lessons taught and benefits received from Stony Brook's athletic program during Frank Gaebelein's administration. Dr. James M. Boice, '56, has said that the most important and lasting lesson he received at Stony Brook was the lesson in perseverence he obtained from his cross-country experience. At Stony Brook the athlete was never led to believe that faith guaranteed victory in the game or race; nor should he pray for victory as a sign of God's favor. The Stony Brook athlete's responsibility has always been to put to best use the conditioning and training he has received and, if he is a Christian, to thank God for the result. "The race is not to the swift, nor the battle to the strong," says the Preacher, and while winning always seems preferable to losing, Stony Brook has tried to teach boys and men alike, through the medium of competitive athletics, that they should expect to profit even from the disappointment of loss.

But if the School overindulged itself in teaching that lesson, to the downgrading and detriment of other phases of learning, it was at fault.

* * *

At the annual meeting of the board of trustees, in December 1959, Dr. Gaebelein informed the board members that it was time for them to begin the search for his successor as headmaster. His retirement was not imminent, but time would be needed to make an unhurried choice. In fact, the task of finding the right man was to take more than two years. Shortly before the School's Fortieth Anniversary Commencement, in the spring of 1962, the board approved the name of Donn Medd Gaebelein, '45, as the next headmaster of The Stony Brook School. His duties would not begin until July 1, 1963; his father would continue as headmaster for the forty-first year.

Despite appearances, the fact that Donn Gaebelein became Stony Brook's second headmaster had nothing to do with filial succession. As far as Frank Gaebelein was concerned, his son had established himself in secondary education in a different form—the country day school—and in a different region—the South. His career there was promising. He had never shown any interest whatsoever in a position at Stony Brook.

"As a father," says Dr. Gaebelein, "I was naturally interested in the board's wish to consider Donn as a candidate. But as the retiring headmaster I could only urge that the best available men be interviewed and that God's guidance be sought in determining the proper choice. I have every confidence that this is precisely what was done."

In the younger Gaebelein, the board was choosing a man who knew Stony Brook as no outsider could possibly know it. Not only had he been raised on the campus as the headmaster's son, but Donn Gaebelein had also been a student fully accepted by his peers. He was not a rebel, but neither was he above accepting a friendly dare. The story of his escapade on the night before the School's Twentieth Anniversary Commencement tells something about the normal boyhood he had enjoyed.

The campus was in a state of anticipation over the ceremonies to be held at the commencement exercises the next day. But two ninth graders, David R. Swanson, '45 (now a Stony Brook trustee) and Donn Gaebelein, were at large looking for a little excitement of their own. On Swanson's urging and dare, Gaebelein took a rock and threw it through the window of Gilbert C. Moore's living room.

It was not a vicious act, merely thoughtless, but in those days such an act of end-of-term exuberance was subject to severe penalties; especially so on this particular occasion, when dignitaries had gathered to mark the School's commemoration. Moore soon had the police, who in turn gave the case back to Dr. Gaebelein as an internal matter.

Frank Gaebelein was apparently in no mood to trifle with vandalism either. He must have made a literal room-by-room investigation, quizzing each boy as to his knowledge of the smashed window. At last he came upon Dave Swanson, who admitted having put someone else up to the deed and who, under pressure no ninth grader on that night could have resisted, identified the culprit.

"About two o'clock in the morning," Donn Gaebelein recalls, "Dad charged into my room upstairs in Grosvenor House, saying, 'Did you do it?' I told him yes, and all that night's frustration broke over my head. Fortunately, my mother came along and cut the violence short just by saying, 'Frank!' I was banished from the School—a punishment that lasted a few hours until P. C. interceded on my behalf later in the day—and condemned to serve 72 hours shoveling coal behind Hegeman Hall.

"I began shoveling early in the morning, but I was interrupted by having to go to the commencement exercises. Then, not having nearly served my sentence, I was transferred along with several other offenders to serve as a waiter at the luncheon for parents and graduates. That was by far the worst part of the punishment. Of course, it was well known what my offense had been, and I felt as though I was the subject of good many *tch-tch*'s and other comments over those tables."

From Stony Brook, Donn Gaebelein had gone to Princeton, majoring in history, and then to Columbia for a master's degree. For two years he had taught English at The McCallie School in Chattanooga, Tennessee. In 1952, he followed Dr. William L. Pressly to a new school in Atlanta, where he had a major role in the development of The Westminster Schools' national prestige.

Westminster's faculty responded to Gaebelein's hard-driving temperament. "As individuals we were a bunch of hot-shots," says Emmett Wright, Jr., now headmaster of the Metairie Park School in New Orleans, "but Donn brought us together and molded our energies and gave us a sense of direction." David T. Lauderdale, Jr.,

Westminster's English Department chairman, says, "Gaebelein has a steel-trap mind. He ran our school out of his hip pocket. I can remember going off for a weekend just before the start of school in the fall, and Gaebelein, he'd swallow a handful of Dramamine to keep off the car-sickness, and in the back seat of the car he'd put together the whole school schedule on pieces of paper spread all over the seat."

Though rumors drifted about the campus throughout the fall, no official word of Dr. Gaebelein's impending retirement reached the faculty as a whole until January 1963. Even then, the new head-master's name was kept from those who were to work with him. The faculty would have to wait until the public announcement at a banquet in New York City, late in April. This strategy was well suited to the purposes of creating a climax of publicity, but the strategy was not well received by the curious faculty, particularly the younger men. They were assured that the board of trustees had chosen carefully and well, but there was an undercurrent of unrest among some who worried that the new headmaster might turn out to be this man or that.

Frank Gaebelein had always carried on his annual negotiations with his teachers during the spring vacation. For many years Stony Brook's faculty have worked by a gentleman's agreement rather than by written contract. A man would be summoned to the headmaster's office in Memorial Hall—or possibly to his study in Grosvenor House—and told of the importance of his contribution to the School, thanked for his past service, and invited to continue for another year at a certain salary. After a momentary pause, the teacher was free to offer his own terms—a change in his teaching responsibilities, perhaps, or a shift in the nature of his nonteaching duties. These talks were seldom lengthy and always concluded with a brief prayer, after which Dr. Gaebelein would rise, step from behind his desk, and gripping the man's hand give him a smile and a shove toward the door.

But the negotiations with the Stony Brook faculty were different in 1963. They began much sooner than the mid-March recess and were conducted in a far deeper philosophical vein than the business-as-usual tone that had characterized them in other years. Now Gaebelein took time to reminisce over the years of a man's association with Stony Brook—what factors had led to his coming to the School, a humorous anecdote that tied the headmaster and his teacher together in some way. Often the course of this discussion turned toward the nature of loyalty—not loyalty to an institution or to a man but to God himself in service to that institution and in cooperation with its appointed head. Again and again he had reminded his faculty that no man is indispensable; now his greatest yearning for his successor was that he should step into the position as headmaster with an experienced and stable faculty to support him.

The final measure of regard for Frank Gaebelein as a leader of men may be the way in which his faculty committed itself to continue the venture into which he had poured his life. The faculty remained almost wholly intact, and as he presided over his final commencement exercises and accepted the title of Headmaster Emeritus, Dr. Frank E. Gaebelein could look back over forty-one years and say:

> In humble recognition of fact, we may say that Stony Brook is the only independent boys' school of good academic standing that not only holds firmly in teaching and worship to evangelical Christianity, as several other good schools do, but is also committed to a faculty made up wholly of regenerated Christians. As such, it is respected by its peers.

To an immeasurable degree the magnitude of that respect continues to be the high regard in which the name of Frank E. Gaebelein is held. As lecturer at colleges and seminaries, as preacher in churches and college chapels, as counselor to various Christian organizations, his word of experience is given special value. But he remains remarkably free of the self-esteem that sometimes afflicts an elder statesman. When he speaks of his experience at Stony Brook, he does so with quiet humility.

"My privilege at Stony Brook was overwhelming," he says in a moment of reflection. "Consider the freedom I was given and the time to work out a Christian philosophy of education. As I think of my failures, I'm rebuked. As I remember all that God has forgiven and overlooked, I'm humbled. And I marvel at the greatness of His love and blessings upon that little school."

What kind of schoolman was Frank Gaebelein? The question remains beyond easy answering. The heroic stature of the man and the breadth of his accomplishment create in different people different responses. Some who worked with him over a period of years found him aloof. One man remembers, for example, Gaebelein's afternoon walks around the outer edge of the campus— a tall figure striding purposefully along, thoroughly oblivious (or so it seemed) to those he passed. At these times he seemed unapproachable, lost in contemplation of some project or problem.

"I'm sure I never really knew the man," says another former colleague. "I first came to Stony Brook as a young boy, and I don't think Gaebelein ever recognized that I had grown up. I never felt that my opinions were respected."

An alumnus who expresses deep gratitude for what he gained from Stony Brook says of Dr. Gaebelein, "I took it for granted that we had nothing in common. He was an intellectual; I felt like a moron by comparison. I expected him to talk about things that were way over my head, and since I had nothing to contribute in conversation with him, I avoided him. I've since discovered that it was my loss."

Some alumni feel that they came to know Dr. Gaebelein well because of some incident during which he gave himself completely to helping them solve a serious problem in their lives. "No one who ever felt that hand on your shoulder and heard him talking with God on your behalf could ever call this man cold," another alumnus declares.

If he gave an impression of brusqueness, it was because the complexities of running a school left him little time for petty affairs, particularly those that he thought he could forestall with a cautioning word. On the morning that a new teacher's first child was born, Dr. Gaebelein went to the teacher's classroom and beckoned him out into the hall. "So, I understand you're a father. Congratulations," he said heartily. Then the other purpose of the conversation: "Just let me remind you that many other couples have brought newborn children into the dormitory without in any way affecting the routine of dormitory life." With that remark, Gaebelein turned and was gone, leaving the teacher bemused for the moment, until he realized that he had been told, in effect, not to demand any special consideration, for either his wife or the infant, from the boys in his dormitory.

A man who has known Frank Gaebelein for more than forty years says, "He was stiff and formal as a younger man. I'm happy to see how much more relaxed and personable he has become later in life. As a matter of fact, it's worth noting that, while most of us tend to become more conservative as we grow older, Frank Gaebelein seems to be much more broad-minded and flexible. It shows in his improved relationships with people.''

Occasionally one meets a Stony Brook graduate who resents what he feels was Dr. Gaebelein's superior air. One such man, now a minister, says, "I always had the feeling that he was looking down on the rest of us from his spiritual pedestal. Yet his theology was outdated. He never taught us anything but personal pietism—no social concern, no awareness of the larger community of Christians who might not quite see eye to eye with Stony Brook, but who were loved of God nonetheless.''

Exactly the opposite reaction comes from another minister who attributes his first sense of deep humility before God to what he saw in Frank Gaebelein and learned by his example. "I went regularly to the Tuesday evening Fellowship meetings in the headmaster's home. It was a great experience to see this man who, we all knew, had such a full experience with God, yet who could kneel with us boys and pray with us about the problems of everyday living.''

Some alumni remember the time Gaebelein came to visit them in the campus infirmary or at one of the nearby hospitals; when he wrote to them during the freshman year at college, encouraging them to maintain a commitment to Christ and to find a regular church in which to worship; or when he stopped by the dormitory room to ask how a particular problem was working out. "I didn't even suppose he knew about it," says another graduate, "and there he was, telling me that he was praying for God's best solution. I'll never forget that!"

Just before Mrs. Gaebelein and he left Stony Brook officially, the Headmaster Emeritus went quietly to each home and dormitory apartment. There he stood briefly at the door, thanking both husband and wife for their help to him and to the School. Then, after praying with them and for them and for Stony Brook, he quickly went on.

This was the lasting impression he left—a man strong in his natural endowments but strongest when at prayer. By this principle he labored, and by this power he led The Stony Brook School to its maturity.

6

Redefining a Christian Community

Tennyson wrote,

> The old order changeth, yielding place to new,
> And God fulfils himself in many ways.

Behind most expressions of good will for Stony Brook's new headmaster, Donn M. Gaebelein, remained this general question, what happens to an institution, particularly a Christian school, when a man the stature of Frank E. Gaebelein moves from the scene?

The answer is that different things happen differently, for each schoolmaster must direct his school according to his own temperament and spiritual insight. Donn Gaebelein is by nature pragmatic. What works best in a given situation, provided that it squares with the ethical dimensions of the problem, will be his method until some better method is discovered.

Gaebelein is also a gambler by temperament. He enjoys watching a plan develop, knowing that he is both anticipating problems and reacting to unexpected complications. He is willing to risk making a mistake in preference to a complacent acceptance of the status quo. His flexibility is like that of a professional quarterback who calls a complex play in the huddle and then, seconds later, changes the play because the defense has shifted. A good administrator recognizes that rigidity is the sure way to disaster.

Gaebelein is also capable of acknowledging a mistake in judgment or in strategy. Perhaps as important, he is also realistic enough to expect less than absolute success. "We have to live with the reality of human error, our own and other people's, sometimes of the most painful kind," he says. "What we gain from our Christian faith is the encouragement to persevere, to pick ourselves up and try again."

This is the spirit in which he undertook the leadership of Stony Brook School. This spirit has characterized his major decisions, the most recent being the introduction of coeducation in 1971. The formal decision, of course, belonged to the board of trustees, but it was through Gaebelein's urging that the decision was reached. Significantly, he waited until both of his own daughters had been graduated from the local public high school before he began his campaign.

The vigor of his imagination at first exceeded that of his faculty. In fact, the committee which he had appointed in 1969 to conduct a preliminary study of the possibilities of admitting girls produced a negative report. In a gesture that shocked some of the faculty, the headmaster thanked the committee for its work, then appointed a second committee to carry the investigation further. From that moment no one at Stony Brook doubted that coeducation would soon come.

"It had to come," says Gaebelein with finality. "The fact of life is this: If a school is going to survive the '70s and '80s and beyond, until the Lord comes, it's going to have to broaden its constituency. Anyone alert to what's happening can tell you that there just aren't going to be enough teenaged boys to fill all the schools in the next twenty years. If a school doesn't adapt to the new pressures of independent education, it's going under."

The new pressures of which Gaebelein speaks are already affecting independent schools, particularly boarding schools. According to the National Association of Independent Schools, many of its member schools are having to face serious threats from three different quarters. Academically the independent school—especially the prestigious Eastern school such as Lawrenceville, Hill, Choate, or Hotchkiss—no longer has the influence it once had in college admissions. When the local American high school was a scholastic wasteland, many ambitious parents were compelled to send their sons away to school. But despite the crisis in the classroom, it must be recognized that in many upper-middle-class neighborhoods public secondary education has raised its standards. In such areas—the well-known instances are Newton, Scarsdale, Evanston Township, and Palo Alto—the suburban high school is a high quality college preparatory school supported by tax dollars.

Furthermore, college admissions practices have greatly changed. Both in recognition of improved public education and in search of greater diversity of students, colleges that once looked first at prep school candidates are now looking elsewhere. Harvard and Yale, traditionally favorable toward "preppies," now have entering classes with fewer than 40 per cent of the students from independent schools.

Financially the continuing downward trend of the American economy has had its effect upon all private schools, for as tuitions have been increased to contend with rising costs, more and more parents have had to withdraw from the market. "It costs a great deal of money to get an independent education," Donn Gaebelein concedes. "Some schools charge in excess of $4000 for tuition alone. To this parents have to add on books, laundry, transportation, spending money." Stony Brook has always charged substantially less than the Eastern average, but in Donn Gaebelein's tenure, since 1963, boarding fees have gone from $1750 to $3300; day student rates from $725 to $1825. "Many families, I know, simply can't afford it," he says. "But what can we do? It still costs us much more per pupil than these tuition fees accrue."

A third pressure reflects a new trend in our society. "Years ago," says Gaebelein, "parents who wanted their children in boarding school said so and the kids went. That's not the way it is anymore. Boys and girls are making that decision today, and in many cases they're deciding to remain at home."

One headmaster, quoted in *The Wall Street Journal,* describes the reasons for rejecting boarding school in blunt terms: "They're weighing the confinement of boarding school against staying home with girls, booze, pot and cars." While this generalization overstates the point, no doubt many potential candidates for boarding school admission are put off by the "Mickey Mouse" regulations and supervision most schools retain as part of their responsibility *in loco parentis.* "The boy who's had the use of the family car all summer isn't going to like being checked in at 11 o'clock at night by his dormitory housemaster," Donn Gaebelein acknowledges. "But that's our obligation, and I don't know many headmasters who make a practice of telling parents that their sons are free to go wherever and whenever they wish.''

These reasons for introducing coeducation are common to all schools, and as many as twenty or more schools this year can be expected to join St. Paul's of Concord, New Hampshire; Loomis, Choate, and Rosemary Hall; or Mount Hermon and Northfield,— schools that have recently "gone coed" or at least combined their resources to achieve the benefits of coeducation. Stony Brook's headmaster cites another reason, however, that influenced his decision.

"In the last few years we've had a large increase in the number of parents of girls asking us, sometimes even pleading with us, to accept their daughters. I always used to reply graciously, I hope, but negatively. Then one day I began to wonder if these negative responses weren't simply arbitrary. Was there any good reason to withhold what Stony Brook has to give a person just because she's a girl?"

Frank Gaebelein recalls that when the School was still in its earliest planning stages there was no thought given to admitting girls with boys. "Not that we had anything inherent against coeducation," he says. "It simply never came into our discussion."

Cultural changes in a half-century, however, convinced Stony Brook's trustees and headmaster that the time had come to enroll girls. As our society has drawn the sexes closer together, at ever earlier ages, it becomes necessary for a school to help make these relationships natural and uncomplicated. As long as girls are scarce and their presence is treated as a phenomenon, boys will tend to regard them as *females* rather than as *persons*. But boys brought into daily experience with girls as fellow students receive a more complete understanding of what girls are. They cease to function merely as objects of attraction, as ornaments to the boy's ego.

Even before the formal introduction to coeducation in 1971, Stony Brook had been working in at least one area to achieve the benefits of mixing boys and girls together. Under the guidance of the chaplain, the Reverend Peter K. Haile, local girls whose commitment to Christ gave them something in common with Christian boys were invited to share in various school activities. Among these were informal Bible studies, tutoring programs for disadvantaged children in the vicinity, and the Stony Brook-Elmendorf Camp. The chaplain has noticed nothing that would bear out the gloomy words of Pope Pius XI, who said, "The so-called method of coeducation is false in theory and harmful to Christian training."

"On the contrary," says Peter Haile, "I believe coeducation more nearly fulfills the ideal of Christian education. I see boys with a new appreciation for the special traits a girl possesses and vice versa. A girl's more natural tenderness for a child's scraped knee, a boy's more natural optimism that this job can be done. For my part of the work here, I wish we'd had coeducation a long time ago."

On September 14, 1971, thirty girls were enrolled in grades eight through eleven. These were not actually Stony Brook's first girl students, although the presence of a few faculty daughters, before the community had its own high school, was scarcely official. One young lady, Pierson Curtis's daughter, Winifred, did make her mark by playing quarterback on the junior school football team. But neither she nor any of the other girls was ever considered for membership in the Alumni Association. Perhaps now their status will be reconsidered.

The present ratio of boys to girls, almost 7 to 2, is not expected to last long. In 1972, girls were admitted as boarding students. Still Gaebelein does not expect enrollment to exceed three hundred. "We want to keep the size of the School at a level we feel our campus can manage comfortably. We may find ourselves someday with a fairly even split between boarders and day students. Certainly that's the trend in our admissions picture."

A statement like this from Gaebelein shows a subtle departure from his father's attitude toward day students. In his annual reports to the board, Frank Gaebelein often might have said something to the effect that the present student body includes *only* 11 day boys or worried that because of insufficient enrollment the School was *forced* to accept 17 day students. "I think my father had a blind spot regarding day students," Donn Gaebelein says. "He believed in the value of the boarder's total involvement; he didn't think that the commuting student could carry away enough of the Stony Brook influence to affect or counteract any unfavorable influences away from school. Frankly, I think he was wrong.

"We find that some of our day students coming, as some do, from only nominally Christian homes, are won to Christ and carry their witness back to their families. And those who are from believing families give us a firm basis of support right here in the community, where we very much need it."

* * *

Donn Gaebelein is a practical man; he is also a man of humble yet profound devotion. He sees the Christian experience from the vantage of the layman, the man in the pew, the man on the job. He has no place in his personal categories for mere spirituality. To him the proof of authentic spirituality lies in action. Thus, his objective as head of a confessing Christian school has been to lead his faculty in discovering fresh ways of demonstrating their Christian faith. In Gaebelein's years as headmaster, he has been particularly gratified by a heightening of Christian character in three distinct areas of Stony Brook's life—in the difficult sphere of personal relationships, in the development of an honor code, and in a widening of Christian testimony.

Early in the fall of 1963, his first year as headmaster, Gaebelein happened upon a group of enraged boys in the junior class. They had just been grilled collectively for an infraction none of them had committed. They were thoroughly bitter, and their expression of frustration made an ugly picture of the School. "I was sure of two things as I listened to them," says Gaebelein. "I was sure the boys were exaggerating, and I was also sure that some of what they claimed was true." Gaebelein had already noted with some concern that most of his faculty held "a rather disturbingly fixed notion of its own rightness" in dealing with a boy's behavior. There was prevalent a spirit of adult moral superiority, something like what Gibbon called "the insolent prerogative of primogeniture."

But Gaebelein also found that the denunciation of adults within the School was rampant. "You can't trust the faculty" was more than a cliche inherited from college protestors, the headmaster learned in conversation after conversation with boys talked to at random. This was also a time when the student revolution was starting to make itself felt in secondary schools as well as colleges. A new set of attitudes among teenagers, an immediate and unhidden questioning of authority—these were manifestations of a new behavior that few adults found easy to accept.

"This was a searching time for many of us," he recalls. "There were good people at Stony Brook who were shocked to learn that their students no longer trusted them, no longer respected them because the boys felt that these men and women had reached their decisions and closed off their minds to further suggestions."

Gaebelein made a commitment: "Before these juniors graduate, in less than two years, we'll turn this picture around."

To do so required the support of the entire faculty, but Gaebelein relied most heavily upon the chaplain, Peter Haile, and Donald W. Marshall, former dean of students, along with Karl E. Soderstrom, who succeeded him. Together these men were commissioned to be *listeners*. Their temperaments ideally suited them to this role. Previously, Stony Brook's counseling had been organized around the admirable but fallacious notion that all Christian teachers were equipped to be counselors. Only the director of studies for academic problems and college placement and the dean for discipline had scheduled time for counseling interviews. The headmaster, of course, handled all major incidents. Stony Brook's counseling services under this arrangement left wide gaps for many boys. Annually each boy was invited to select some man with whom he felt affinity, but the breakdown in such a system can readily be imagined.

Gaebelein reduced teaching assignments and provided competent assistance for their other work so that Haile, Marshall and now Soderstrom were able to devote the bulk of their days to conferences with boys and girls. Most of these conferences are voluntarily arranged by the student wishing to discuss some problem. At other times the chaplain may choose to take the initiative in talking to a student about a problem brought to his attention. For example, it is not unusual for a boy or girl from a theologically (and perhaps politically) conservative home to feel a tension growing between familiar home teachings and new ideas learned at school. Troubled by these thoughts, the student may seek out Peter Haile.

"In counseling sessions like these," he says, "I always try to show a genuine understanding for what the parents and home churches have stood for. But I also try to impart an appreciation for the teenager's doubts and questions. I try to help him distinguish between the essentials of biblical Christianity and the mere cultural accretions added down through the years. Most of all, I try to encourage him to express his new ideas in a way that will be loving to his parents."

Once in a while such parents also require counseling—as when a father, whose politics were slightly to the right of the Ku Klux Klan, accused the School of undermining his son's faith with communism because his boy no longer believed that blacks were cursed by God to be the servants of white men.

In other counseling situations, the boy or girl is called to the dean's office because Soderstrom has received a report of an infraction. The School treats such a report as a serious matter and encourages the faculty to make every effort to deal with disciplinary problems on the level of teacher-to-pupil. Some Stony Brook teachers are proud of never having passed along a routine report; others seem to send an unending flow.

"When I get such a report," says Soderstrom, a 6'5" basketball coach, "I have to regard it as already being in the nature of a failure between some teacher and this boy or girl. If the teacher had succeeded, I might never have known about this case. My first job, then, is to try to get through all the emotional overlays—the anger of the teacher, the humiliation and resentment of the student—and down to reality. What went wrong between these two people? This means that I rely a good deal on the answers to questions, and I try to make it very clear that my judgment depends on what kind of picture I see drawn for me by the words the boy or girl uses to describe the situation."

From such a counseling interview Soderstrom may learn that the student has a deep emotional problem, to which the outburst in class may or may not be related. He may also learn that this particular student was mishandled by an adult who ought to have been more patient in dealing with the teenager. "I can't say that I've ever counseled with a student who was absolutely innocent. But I've counseled with lots of kids who were no more guilty of thoughtlessness or stubbornness than the person who turned them in."

Soderstrom's job is primarily counseling, secondarily punitive. But he feels that some of his best relationships, over the years he has been the dean of students, have been with boys to whom he has had to administer the most severe punishment. "Of course, penalties are given only after the student and I have talked about ways to redeem the broken relationship," Soderstrom says. "We believe here that penalties are important, not as a show of force but because a penalty affirms the worth of the student. It tells him that his actions are important; what he does matters."

Soderstrom refuses to tie in punishment with sermonizing. "I don't really believe that it's appropriate for me to dish out a penalty that consists of eight hours of physical work, plus the loss of off-campus privileges for the weekend, and then turn around and begin lecturing about the love of God and the forgiveness of Christ."

Soderstrom prefers a follow-up conversation sometime after the student has been penalized. "Then I feel I have a chance to dig into problems of motivation or aimlessness or self-rejection, which so often lead to behavior problems. It's out of conversations like these that real healing and strengthening take place."

Karl Soderstrom's primary training has been in theology; since taking over the office of dean of students, he has also received a master's degree in counseling. But his great asset is not what he knows but who he is. In spite of his potentially odious role as disciplinarian, no man at Stony Brook is held in greater affection. "I can talk to him," says a usually taciturn boy, words of high praise indeed.

Counseling for improved relationships also extends to problems of larger social dimension, for Stony Brook has carried on Frank Gaebelein's commitment to open its doors to deserving students of every race. The character of the student body is distinctly cosmopolitan, with students from some twenty or more foreign countries each year. The Class of 1972, for instance, included a Montagnard boy from South Vietnam, Ha Kin Lieng. He had been at Stony Brook since the eighth grade, sponsored jointly by Project Concern, the local Jaycees, and the School.

By far the largest and most visible minority bloc, of course, is the black students. Since 1966, a larger number of blacks has been admitted each year so that in 1972, the School has nearly 30 blacks, 7 of whom are girls, in a student enrollment of about 270.

Although the black students have begun to gain respect as leaders (a recent senior class president was a black; the 1971-72 Honor Committee chairman was also a black), most blacks have been reluctant to move beyond athletics as a means of achieving status in the School. When one of the group, a Martin Luther King, Jr., Scholarship holder, tried out for a part in a school play and won the role, he was criticized by some of "the brothers." "I told them," he says, "this is my school, too. There's nothing in the handbook that says no black man can be in a play. I want to leave this place knowing I can make it in something besides sports."

The cultural problems facing blacks or any other minority group entering a primarily white community for the first time are numerous. They may also appear to be remarkably trivial. As an example, the matter of dietary differences has caused sharp complaints from some blacks that "this school is trying to force a white man's appetite on us" by insisting on each student's eating regular portions of foods common to most institutions. Hair styles and the mustache as an assertion of masculinity are also topics of some complaint. One black, an avowed Muslim, was so attached to his incipient mustache that he periodically nicked his upper lip while shaving. The wound required only a Band-Aid but carried with it the nurse's dispensation against further shaving.

At Stony Brook, as elsewhere in America, it seems increasingly difficult for the black student to merge quietly into the student body. A junior, a spokesman among the blacks, says, "You see, man, it's like we always feel somehow we're being watched special. Most of us are on a scholarship here—from the School or a church or a foundation. We know they got ways of finding out which one of us is getting out of line and isn't going to be invited back here next year. We just don't feel too inconspicuous, know what I mean?"

"Some of the teachers don't make me feel all that comfortable either," says another junior with a blossoming Afro hair style. "Like, when we're all sitting around a table in the dining room after dinner and this one teacher keeps looking over at us, looking and looking, real nervous. So one of the brothers calls over, 'Hey, Mr. So-'n-so, why don't you come and join us? We're planning a revolution.' Man, that cat couldn't believe his ears. He had heard what he expected to hear and he couldn't believe it himself when he heard it!"

One of the irritants blacks complain of is the assumption on the part of whites in general that reduces blackness to an easy sociological formula: *black* means *ghetto* means *deprivation*. One of the blacks in the senior class puts it this way: "Some of these people hear that I come from Newark or Harlem or some place like that and to them that automatically means I got to live in some tenement. Now, I don't mean that I live in no palace, but we've got a clean house. My father and mother live together, they both work, we don't live on welfare. But some of these people think because I'm black, they've got to raise me up out of some awful mess at home. They never stop to wonder if maybe I got something to contribute from my blackness—something that might make Stony Brook a better place for them!"

In its classrooms Stony Brook has begun to recognize the significance of African history and of black literature with special courses being taught in both. When the black literature elective course was first offered to a class with only one black student out of fifty-three, the School showed clearly that it was not merely trying to appeal to a vocal minority; it was interested in acquainting its students with the work of writers as yet unfamiliar to them. A white teacher conducted the course, although there was a black man in the English Department. This too was deliberate, contesting the popular assumption that to appreciate black literature one must qualify through "the black experience."

"We haven't accepted that proposition," says Mark Hanchett, a 1962 Stony Brook alumnus and teacher of the course. "By the same reasoning you'd have to be a murderer, or at least a Scot, to appreciate Macbeth's predicament. One of the essential distinctions of *literature* is its universality. The best literature written by black men and women touches me, a white man, because it's art. Inferior writing by white men and women leaves me unmoved, even though I too am white, because it's trash."

Stony Brook has found that social problems in America at large cannot be kept at bay. While dormitory housing does not seem to be a serious issue—blacks and whites share rooms without question or incident—the problem of dating is another matter. The black boy and girl in a predominantly white social situation have a frustrating time. "In my first year," Laurence Foster, Jr., '57, the first black alumnus, recalls, "a date was found for me to the first school-wide party. I didn't attend any other parties with a date thereafter. One must remember that it is in this social area that many of the greatest problems of racial integration originally develop."

With only a few black girls in the student body, for parties today the School relies on the availability of black girls from towns fifteen or twenty miles away. The proximity of the campus to Stony Brook's black community on Christian Avenue has had no great benefit for black students. "Man, I was in this school for three years," says a senior, "before I even knew there was a black community just about two miles away. And it's old, man! It's been here for three hundred years. So Stony Brook is my town too. But we don't see much of those people. In fact, some of the brothers consider them *country* people, you know?"

Some mixed dating occurs, and Stony Brook has no official position on the matter. As far as one black student is concerned, "I think the School worries too much about black and white dating. I mean, we're not all that eager to date white girls, we'd just like to date *some* girls. I think the School could do more to see that there are girls for us, if it's all that important."

At the base of these and other problems is the need for an identity and the self-assurance such an identity provides. The black student at Stony Brook, as at other boarding schools, often finds himself cut off from familiar surroundings. The entire milieu is foreign to him, the expectations of the community are more than he wishes to concede. As Silberman points out, many black students refuse to pay that price. Yet, he also says, "to some degree, their refusal may be naive and unrealistic; if education does *not* force a student to question his background, if it does not give him the means to live comfortably in cultures other than his own, it is not really education."

"Naive" and "unrealistic" are epithets easily applied, but the problem for some ghetto blacks away at a school like Stony Brook for the first time runs much deeper than surface accusations can account for. "I don't know nothing about white people," said a black newly arrived at Stony Brook. "Where I live a white man doesn't walk down my street. It's not healthy." The bitterness of generations of oppression already blights such a human being before he has an opportunity to learn about personal relationships with whites for himself. How different the understanding of another black, whose home environment is just as hostile to whites but who has been at Stony Brook two years longer than the first student: "I'll tell anybody who asks me that one thing being at Stony Brook has taught me is that maybe black is beautiful but *black* isn't the only way to spell *brother.* I know a lot of white guys who I respect as people, and I know they respect me as a man. I am a black man, but I got to be respected as a man first."

Attaining self-respect and respect from one's peers is doubly hard for the young person who lives in two different worlds and who feels like an outlander in both. Some of the hardest problems the black student has to face are not at school but at home, while he is on recess from Stony Brook. Most blacks complain that they feel cut off from their friends, even from members of their families. One boy feels so estranged from his community, he stays in his apartment over most of a two-week vacation. "It takes me weeks in the summer to feel free to go down to the local playground. All the people on my block know I go to a prep school—they call it a 'honky school'—and they don't like it."

Occasionally a black student has admitted having to resort to disloyal but (in his circumstances) perfectly understandable measures to regain lost status in the neighborhood. This usually means criticizing or "bad-mouthing" the School and ridiculing its principles. "I've done it," a sophomore from Bedford-Stuyvesant says, "and I feel real bad while I'm doing it and worse when I'm done. I don't mean it. I really like Stony Brook. But, man, you got to understand, things are real different in there. You got to know how to survive."

The struggle to survive, to this student, means compromising with black bigotry. In time, like others, he may learn how to retain his ethnic identity and dignity while at the same time being flexible toward new experiences. To a large degree the Orientals at Stony Brook have succeeded in doing this. They move with apparent freedom from mixed relationships to speaking in Chinese or Japanese with a fellow countryman. They drop their national differences to collaborate on a sumptuous dinner for the faculty marking the Chinese New Year. Together they constitute the most scholastically aggressive bloc in the School.

Perhaps one reason why Stony Brook's blacks have not generally felt comfortable in the school environment is because few, as yet, have been academically successful. Stony Brook is a college preparatory school; as such its greatest pressures for achievement come from its academic side. This is true for all students. Laurence Foster, Jr., remembers that "although the general prep school pressure to succeed was apparent, my Stony Brook experience was possibly not much different for me as a Negro from that of my schoolmates."

The pressure, however, is greatest upon the student with a weak supporting background in study habits or in verbal skills. Some of Stony Brook's blacks score only in the upper-300s and low-400s on the Scholastic Aptitude Test. For some of their failure to achieve, the School is at fault in failing to give adequate remedial work that would bring disadvantaged yet potentially able students up to a level of accomplishment. The School has chosen instead a policy similar to Daniel P. Moynihan's "benign neglect." Not wishing to create virtually all-black remedial classes, Stony Brook has chosen to keep many of its courses heterogeneously grouped. Only those courses presumably leading toward the Advanced Placement program are grouped by ability.

The typical black student, therefore, is left to swim for his academic life. Some respond well to the challenge; others do not. Individual help, of course, is available from teachers but there is not enough time to do the necessary job. And, in fairness, it must be added that like all teenagers, regardless of color, many of those who most need academic help rarely appear voluntarily when it is offered.

Another reason for the typical black student's uneasiness at Stony Brook is a consensus throughout the younger black American community that Christianity is "the white man's religion" and an instrument of oppression. Columbus Salley and Ronald Behm explain the argument carefully in their book, *Your God Is Too White:*

> Because of the negative impressions prevalent among a significant number of blacks concerning the ability of "Christianity" to meet this need [for a right standing before a holy and loving God that is common to all men], every independent-thinking black person must examine the original source of the Christian religion and then determine whether or not his need for a right standing with God is met by the Christian God— not the white God of racist "Christianity."

"It took me a while to learn that this place is different," says a thoughtful black student who has been at Stony Brook for four years. "Sure, anybody who really wanted to pick holes could say, 'Oh yea, it's a racist institution because it doesn't have this and it doesn't do that.' But I leave that kind of nit-picking to the militants.

I know what's true for me, and that is that I'm getting a good education, I've made some friends, and I've found an experience with God that is real to me. I'd like to see some attitudes change, mostly in people who don't recognize how little things can hurt. But I've got to say that there are real Christians here."

For its part, Stony Brook has attempted to meet the issue of Christianity as "the white man's religion" in a straightforward fashion. Two of the most effective speakers to visit the campus, for week-long evangelistic meetings and personal counseling, are Tom Skinner and William Pannell, black evangelists. Pastors of black students' home churches have been guest preachers for Sunday services.

"We've also encouraged our black students to take a leading part in activities such as the Stony Brook-Elmendorf Camp," Peter Haile says. "By doing something that shares their faith with somebody else, people learn the true meaning of *community*. And the true meaning of *community* automatically eliminates any idea that Jesus Christ belongs exclusively to this group or that. He doesn't belong to us; we who serve him belong to him!"

* * *

A natural consequence of Donn Gaebelein's search for greater openness within the School was the beginning of an honor system in 1967. The idea for an honor code was not new at Stony Brook; it had been proposed before but had never gained acceptance until the suggestion came from the students, in particular from a group led by David V. Hicks, '66, who was to become Stony Brook's first Rhodes Scholar. A committee of faculty and students met for a year, reading the regulations governing honor systems in other schools and visiting such schools as Woodberry Forest in Virginia and the Pingry School in New Jersey.

No one thought it would be easy to sell Stony Brook on the idea of an honor system. Many boys are taught that so-called honor systems are merely fascist devices for legalized talebearing. Like Billy Budd, many boys possess an "erring sense of uninstructed honor" that protects an offender for fear of peer disapproval. To persuade students otherwise, Stony Brook's approach from the outset was to stress the biblical truth that each of us is his brother's keeper. Each is therefore responsible before God to help his brother, to snatch him back from a dangerous situation rather than allowing him to persist. Helping the dishonorable offender to be aware of his hurt to himself became the object of Stony Brook's honor code.

In the spring of 1967, Stony Brook's students elected over-whelmingly to enter upon a trial period, during which the honor code was in effect. The terms of the code confined it at first to academic cheating. Each boy was required to pledge his honor by affirming in writing, "I have neither given nor received any aid on this examination." Violators were reported to the Honor Committee, elected by the students, with a faculty adviser selected by the committee. At the end of the year, the student body once again voted in favor of the honor system, and it became permanent in the fall of 1967.

The chairman of the Honor Committee that year was Stephen B. Jamison, '68, an unusually mature and impressive young man who seemed more like a father-figure than a schoolmate to some of his fellows. Jamison gave the new system a dignity it needed in its initial full year. The minority of students who still worried about the honor system's being used as another faculty club over their heads found that Jamison and his committee were both fair and summary in their judgments. There was no wheedling with this group; there was no self-righteousness either. The committee had power to summon an accused offender to appear in private and answer the charges against him. Then the committee could discipline the offender, if judged guilty on incontrovertible evidence, in any of several ways: by reprimand, by probation with a warning of suspension for any future violation, by recommending a brief suspension, or an outright separation from the School, in which case the headmaster was called upon to administer the verdict.

In one case during that year, a sophomore was found guilty of cheating. Jamison wrote to the boy's father, a businessman in a Great Lakes city, requesting that he come to Stony Brook to meet with the Honor Committee regarding his son's problem. The father came with some skepticism over a boy's handling so major a responsibility; he left with words of high praise for the spirit in which he had been received and the compassion he felt had been expressed toward his son. That boy graduated two years later as one of the most reliable members of his class, his past mistake com-pletely erased by the record he had since established.

Recently, the honor code has been expanded so that it now covers the whole area of personal property. Theft is one of the scourges of any boarding school. Nothing demoralizes a dormitory's sense of family like the knowledge that someone in the house is a thief. Stony Brook has always insisted on an open door to each dormitory room, but many boys have had to resort to strong boxes for their valuables. Even so, each year brings one or two expulsions for stealing. Both Donn Gaebelein and Karl Soderstrom hope that the new emphasis upon a relationship between theft and the violation of one's honor will help those teenagers who have treated stealing lightly.

A freshman boy who had been caught in a web of petty stealing from stores in the neighborhood came to Soderstrom, admitting what he had done and asking for help. The dean put the boy in his car and drove him from store to store. Together they faced the merchant in each business and explained the boy's intention to make good on his thefts. In every case the store owners were happy to co-operate. Next, Soderstrom helped the student to locate paying jobs to earn the money he needed. Before the year was out, the boy had repaid his debts.

"We've concentrated a lot of energy," Gaebelein says in a thoughtful tone, "on trying to show that our motto, *'Character before Career,'* is really a statement about attitudes. A man's attitudes toward the several aspects of his world makes up his character. What is it that Aristotle says? 'Character is what shows a man's disposition—the kind of things he chooses or rejects when his choice is not obvious.' Honor is one part of character, and so a man's attitude toward honor is really a reflection of his character. But when that character becomes imbued by the Spirit of God, then we can expect that the choices will become somewhat more obvious—between what will or will not conform to the principles of Scripture."

Along with this increased emphasis upon personal honor has come a new slant on the individual's responsibility to his community. Whereas in the past Stony Brook's students knew that certain violations of school rules would be treated "by the book," they now know that each major disciplinary case is treated individually and with greater regard for the student's responsibility. Once, getting caught smoking or drinking meant an almost automatic one-week or two-week suspension, whereas lying might mean a series of heart-to-heart talks with the dean or chaplain. Now Stony Brook treats its miscreants differently. Smoking and drinking are still forbidden, but today's violator may serve his penalty at

Stony Brook rather than at home; he continues his schoolwork without the privileges of off-campus permission, without the holiday of a week or two at home. By contrast, the boy caught stealing or lying is treated much more seriously than before. A deliberate and calculated scheme constructed out of lies receives, perhaps, the most serious penalty Stony Brook can give—immediate separation from the School.

"The boys themselves came to us with this proposal," says Karl Soderstrom. "They felt that we were holding on too tightly to a penalty structure that glamorized social taboos—actions like smoking and drinking. Here we were, talking about honor and a sense of responsibility to the community, yet not treating the violations of trust as stiffly as we treated some kid's puffing on a cigarette behind the fieldhouse. It seemed inconsistent to them and seems so to us."

The same attitude has governed Stony Brook's response to drug experimentation. How many of Stony Brook's students have experimented with the illegal use of drugs, no one is prepared to say. The number of known cases has been few, even though the School and town suffered the notoriety of a police raid on the campus of the State University at Stony Brook in January 1968. In the sloppy fashion that fails to distinguish *university* or *college* from *school,* news broadcasts at the time referred to the university as "the school at Stony Brook," thereby alarming people all over the country who knew Stony Brook School. Even three years later, a father in Maine was reluctant to send his boy to Stony Brook because he remembered having heard about the drug raid "at that school."

But while the incident did no good for Stony Brook's public image, it did awaken the administration to the prevalence of drug use in the area and to the easy availability through various sources. The next edition of the *Student Handbook* contained this additional statement:

Drugs

Taking or possessing drugs or marijuana is against Federal law and will subject the student to dismissal, as well as to appropriate legal action.

Each instance of drug violation since then has been treated individually. In 1970, for example, a group of boys was found smoking marijuana in Hegeman Hall. They were treated as abusers of the common trust placed in them as members of the community.

Privatism resulting from the need to hide one's actions, they were told, leads to the breakdown of relationships. They would have to withdraw from the school community for a lengthy enough period to give themselves a chance to review their attitudes toward Stony Brook, to ask themselves whether or not they wished to belong again to a community that expected this much of them.

Some of the offenders asked to address the assembled School in the morning chapel service just before they left the campus. It was a highly emotional moment, but each boy made his voluntary statement with reasonableness and composure. The audience of schoolmates and teachers was deeply affected.

Donn Gaebelein consulted his faculty before deciding on the permanent disposition of this case. At first, faculty sentiment ran strongly against allowing any of the group to resume their places at Stony Brook. They had despoiled the School; they had reduced Stony Brook to being just another school where boys traffic in drugs, and so on. Gradually, however, this attitude reversed itself as the teaching of forgiveness, particularly as dramatized in the parable of the Prodigal Son, impressed itself upon these men and women. Influencing them were penitent letters from three of the suspended students. After more than a month's absence, all three were welcomed to return; two others were not. Interestingly, one of the three who returned and both of those who did not have since reported that during this experience they committed their lives in faith to Jesus Christ.

A later incident of drug abuse resulted in the offending students' voluntary withdrawal from Stony Brook altogether. One of them wrote an open letter to the headmaster and "all others concerned," in which he said:

> I have not been honest with the School or myself since September and I don't think I could have lasted much longer the way it was. I still am very much concerned with the School; this is why I am resigning. . . .
>
> Drugs cannot be a part of a community like Stony Brook; I hope it will never be one. Drugs assume a certain falseness which cannot prevail at a school such as this. . . .
>
> It is regrettable that I took drugs in the first place, but it is good that I have been stopped by people who care.

*   *   *

Foster Q. Doan of Westtown School, speaking before a meeting of the Council for Religion in Independent Schools, has said, "We talk easily about 'new math' and now 'new English.' Are chapel programs keeping pace? Is the worship in our chapels reflective of the crisis of contemporary life, or does it reflect the more cloistered existence of a bygone era?" To this question Donn Gaebelein has addressed much of his energy as headmaster—to making the ministry of The Stony Brook School, through its chapel program, a natural outgrowth of the Christian's daily experience with Jesus Christ.

The School meets for a daily worship service in Hegeman Memorial Chapel each morning, Monday through Friday, and on Sundays. Separate daily chapel services for older and younger students are ten to fifteen minutes long and consist of a hymn, an invocation, a talk by a teacher or a student, and a benediction. Once each week this pattern is set aside for a period of group singing. The Sunday morning hour blends several standard orders of worship to include the Lord's Prayer, Apostles' Creed, and the singing of the *Gloria* and the *Doxology.* Sunday's preachers are usually distinguished pastors, missionaries, or educators, with an occasional Christian layman.

Recently, however, significant changes in worship methods have been introduced. A litany written by a student, a Scripture reading in contemporary language from a worshipper seated in the congregation, or the sermon early in the service with appropriate music and public testimony following—these are a few of the variations. To these changes, Stony Brook's faculty has given its wholehearted support.

The whole subject of faculty support for the chapel program, in schools that maintain it, has been a sticky one. In *A World of Our Own,* Peter S. Prescott notes that only a handful of Choate's faculty attend the chapel; other schools report the same. At Stony Brook, the policy is clearly stated by the headmaster to the faculty: "We are present at the daily chapel service unless providentially detained." Then Gaebelein adds, "I recognize that some of us have a broader view of providence than others, and I leave that to your conscience and discretion."

In fact, Stony Brook's faculty gives a high degree of support to the daily services. No attendance check is made of teachers as is done with students—except the check made by curious students who crane their necks each morning in order to spot the absentees.

Perhaps the most provocative change in worship, and the one that has caused the most discussion among faculty, has been in the location and manner of Communion services. As chaplain, Peter Haile has increased the number of celebrations of the Lord's Supper to one a month, whereas Frank Gaebelein had held only one or two each term. Some of these services are held, as before, in Hegeman Chapel; others meet elsewhere.

It is 8:45 on a Tuesday night, with classes as usual scheduled for the next day. The lobby of Monro Hall is crowded nonetheless with a little over a hundred persons, most of them students, some faculty and spouses. They are crowded around a metal folding table on which has been set a single loaf of bread and tiny glasses of grape juice. These glasses in their silver trays are the only reminder of the customary Communion practice.

A celebration of the Lord's Supper has been announced; these people have come together to share their faith and fellowship in Jesus Christ.

Between interruptions to point out vacant seats to late arrivals, Chaplain Peter Haile speaks informally to the gathering. "It's important to know who we are and why we're here tonight. We are the old and young, the simple and the intellectual, the good and—yes—the bad too. We're here not because we are old and intellectual and good, not because we are young and simple and bad, but because we know who Jesus is and because we want to declare our love for him and for others. We're not here to judge others who are also here; we're not here to judge others who aren't here. We are here to know Jesus better."

Then Peter Haile suggests that anyone who wishes to share his faith do so by speaking about his own experience, by quoting a passage of Scripture, by suggesting a hymn (hymnals from the chapel have been provided), or by offering a brief prayer. There is surprisingly little hesitancy, almost no indication of reticence. A senior begins by saying, "Some times I really wonder if Jesus is real in my life, but then I remember how rotten I felt before I came to know him and how good I feel now. So I know he must be real."

A junior cross-country champion speaks from his experience as a runner. He had neglected to report back at Stony Brook for the voluntary early track practice during the last week of spring vacation. As a result he finds himself behind in his training. "I hurt all over because I'm not in good condition; I got away from regular training during the vacation. It's just like that with my relationship with God. If I say to Him, 'Go away, I don't want to see you today,' I soon find that I'm out of shape. Just like I have to run every day, so I have to keep my familiarity with God on a daily basis."

Another speaker testifies about his present state of mind and soul. "The key word for me this spring is *doubt*. It all started, like every important Christian experience is supposed to, at a week-end conference! I went to the Buck Hill Falls conference of the Council for Religion in Independent Schools, and there I met a lot of kids who were thinking thoughts I'd never bothered to investigate. I'd always been taught that doubting was a form of weakness, so I'd been afraid to ask myself these questions before. But I found that doubting didn't cause me to lose my faith. It only gave me the opportunity to examine new forms of truth. I now look at doubting as a direct means of growth."

In between these and other affirmations are requests for hymns. Although Stony Brook has sponsored many folk and rock music services, contemporary spiritual songs have not caught on generally. The hymns requested are shockingly old-fashioned—"Praise to the Lord the Almighty," "O Jesus Thou Art Standing," "Great Is Thy Faithfulness," "Praise Him, Praise Him, Jesus Our Blessed Redeemer." The singing is lusty and enthusiastic.

Peter Haile stands at the table and tears the loaf of bread, reminding the group that the body of Jesus was torn and broken for each of them. The four sections are distributed throughout the room, each person taking a small piece of the loaf, waiting to eat it until all have been served. Later the glasses of grape juice are passed about, the chaplain reminding the communicants that "this wine is in token of the shed blood of Jesus, as well as representing the new life he offers by his death and resurrection."

A final prayer of benediction concludes the service, and the chaplain invites each person to greet those on either side of himself and to "go in joy and peace."

Services of this type are not unusual at Stony Brook. At one time some of the School's faculty would have felt squeamish about removing the sacrament of Holy Communion to a dormitory lounge. The reality of faith expressed in these informal, yet sacred, moments has by this time removed most reservations. It has also helped other teachers and students to think of new ways of putting faith into practice. One teacher banded together some of the School's strongest boys—boys who also seemed only marginally approachable on spiritual matters. This group of eight or nine took the first week after the end of school to travel into New England and there work at opening up three Christian conference grounds. They cleared away brush, repaired broken docks, patched roofs, and generally put things in order.

"We worked hard all day," says John Engstrom, football coach and leader of the work force, "and we'd sit around a fire and talk at night about the Lord and different questions these guys had about Christianity. We didn't talk long—we were too bushed for that—and I never lectured, but I think we made some progress."

Another teacher has used a different method. An avid skier, he organizes week-end ski trips to various sites in the Northeast, keeping the cost down by turning a school van into a traveling dormitory with bunk beds. The purpose is to enjoy skiing but also to bring people into a relationship that makes it possible to talk seriously about life and the claims of Jesus Christ.

Edwin A. Rian has said, "A Christian theory of education is an exposition of the idea that Christianity is a world and life view and not simply a series of unrelated doctrines. . . . Christianity is not something to add to the curriculum nor a department which needs only to be enlarged to be effective. Christianity is the basis and the unifying philosophy of the whole educational program." At Stony Brook this means that Christianity is to be demonstrated by an adherence to sound doctrine in the chapel and in the academic classes in Bible; it means that the sacrament of Holy Communion is to be celebrated in remembrance of Christ's passion and death. But it also means that Christianity is to be demonstrated by a man's relationship with a group of boys on a ski week end; by a faculty wife's hospitality in welcoming a cluster of girls and boys into the dormitory apartment; by a couple's decision to take a homeless boy as their ward; by the willingness of the student body to give up meat at meals for a specified period, the proceeds to be credited to the Stony Brook-Elmendorf Camp; by the willingness of Norma

Gaebelein, the headmaster's wife, to turn her home into a recital hall or recreation center.

"The New Testament tells us quite plainly," says Gaebelein, "that pure religion is a lot more than piousness. Christian character is founded on faith, but Christian character is expressed in works. As a Christian school Stony Brook is committed to teaching both elements of character."

The question may well be asked, "After fifty years what keeps Stony Brook true to its founders' aims?" Other schools have started out with similar objectives; their charters, chapels, and mottoes testify to their original intent. Yet in far less time than a half-century most of these schools have veered from that course. The charter has been interpreted in a new light, the chapel has become an assembly hall, and the motto has declined into a mere slogan. What makes Stony Brook different?

Stony Brook has remained constant to its declared purposes for several reasons. In the first place, those purposes are grounded, the School believes, upon the Person of Jesus Christ himself, who is "the same, yesterday, today, and forever." If an institution or an individual wishes to commit itself or himself to the service of Christ, there must follow a commitment to constancy. One does not serve the Son of God this week and the alumni association or the National Merit Scholarship program the next week. The Christian school has its purpose laid out clearly in the words of St. Paul to young Timothy, "Study to shew thyself approved unto God."

Such an unwavering purpose does not, however, restrict the Christian school from varying its methods. A school built upon the dynamic foundation of Jesus Christ, who is Truth, can accept change. "Change on an unstable foundation," Frank Gaebelein has said, "may be perilous, but change based on the revelation of God's truth through Christ and the Bible can bring great progress, provided that it is compatible with the Christian way of life set forth in the Scriptures." Stony Brook is not the same school today that it was fifty years—or even fifty weeks—ago. It has changed in personnel and in method; but it has not changed in character.

The reason for its firmness of character lies in the single most unique feature about the School: the unity of a faculty committed in personal faith to Jesus Christ. This faith, held in accord by each teacher, accounts for another reason why Stony Brook remains true to its charter and its Platform of Principles. Because this faith is practiced as well as professed, it makes itself evident in every phase of school life; it is not confined to faculty prayer meetings or well-prepared chapel talks.

Furthermore, because the Christian faith of the Stony Brook faculty is an individual experience, rather than a creedal assent, it expresses itself differently in the life of each person. In one teacher, the student sees a genuine spirit of cheeriness in spite of circumstances; in another, the student sees a depth of loving concern that encourages trust and confidence; in still another, the student observes a thoroughness in the performance of routine tasks and a joy in their accomplishment; and in yet another, the student witnesses a keen awareness of the needs of others and a readiness to be helpful.

Stony Brook's faculty has no party line, no canned speeches to give concerning the Christian faith. In its recent faculty meetings, during which the whole philosophy and practice of the School have been given a golden anniversary review, various exchanges of opinion have been straightforward, pointed though not personal, and spoken in tones that reveal an intense concern for the School's future. Yet, while much of what has previously served as a statement of philosophy and objectives has been subjected to revision, this revision has only been to articulate even more clearly than before the fidelity of the Stony Brook faculty to its historic purposes. There is no question of discarding this or that tenet of faith as an idea now outworn. At Stony Brook today as in 1922 and before, the Word of God is still the unshakable basis. By no other means can a Christian school retain its integrity of purpose.

7

A Vision of Greatness

When a school like Stony Brook passes the milestone of its fiftieth year, it is natural to pause and ask, "What of the future? Where is such a school heading?" Perhaps it is more to the point to inquire, "In what direction should such a school go to fulfill its mission as a Christian school?" All attempts to see into the future must begin with a look at the present and, eventually, at the past, for as the Preacher said, "That which is, already has been; that which is to be, already has been."

First, the present. In education we see confusion and contradiction, "an age of crisis," Silberman calls it. The paradoxes are confounding. At a time when the world has shrunk through jet travel and satellite television, American education seems to be withdrawing into a vacuum of solipsism. The world at large, comprehended in the past through the study of history, literature, and foreign languages, is no longer relevant to the typical secondary school curriculum. Today's offerings are studies in the poetry of popular song lyrics, 8 mm film-making, and other narrow pursuits. There is almost never a course in geography—political, economic, or old-fashioned states-capitals-rivers-mountains.

In colleges the phobia of learning anything older than yesterday's headlines calls for courses in the *Playboy* philosophy of Hugh Hefner, the close analysis of *Mad* magazine, or yoga as a channel to inner fulfillment. The nature of this anti-intellectualism is described by Theodore Roszak in *The Making of A Counter-Culture:*

> Often enough, such madcap brainstorming under the auspices of instructors hardly out of their teens degenerates into a semiarticulate, indiscriminate celebration of everything in sight that is new, strange, and noisy; a fondling of ideas that resembles nothing so much as an infant's play with bright, unfamiliar objects.

In schools the same fad attempts to dignify itself with jargon— "phase electives" meaning "mini-courses" consisting of two or three weeks' dabbling in profound subjects or, worse, the same time spent at making the shallow appear profound. The result is often mini-effort and mini-learning by mini-minds.

This parlous state in education, with its exaltation of trivia, threatens to destroy whatever remains of American education's right to free inquiry. For whenever genuine intellectualism allows itself to be diverted into foolishness, the inevitable reaction of philistine authority is to strike out in ways that inhibit responsible free inquiry.

Already we are seeing evidence of imposition upon education in the two-pronged attack of behavioral science and cut-the-budget politicians. This attack takes the form of mandates compelling teachers to express their teaching objectives solely in behavioral terms. By so restricting the teacher, the behavioral psychologist is pleased: he achieves an easy measurement for his library of statistics. The economy-minded school board member is also pleased: he foresees the elimination of a lot of "frills" that cannot be measured and therefore no longer belong in the curriculum— frills such as the growing acquisition of *taste* in art and literature or the development of *character* in performing some difficult learning task.

All this is to say that we have entered upon the burgeoning of Jacques Ellul's "technological state." In the early 1950s, the Protestant scholar Ellul in France and Joseph Wood Krutch, an agnostic in America, warned their readers of the fate awaiting those who unwarily turn over their bodies, minds, and souls to amoral scientism. Under the influence of laboratory-minded clinicians, education has become more and more a *process,* less and less a search. The behaviorism of B.F. Skinner, the taxonomies of Robert F. Mager, W. James Popham, Benjamin S. Bloom, and others, the "systems approach" to learning have done what they can to reduce the human experience to a passel of predetermined expectations.

In *The Measure of Man,* Krutch summarized the problem this way:

As influence, power, and authority in our society pass, as they are passing, from philosophers and theologians into the hands of those who call themselves "human engineers" whether they happen to be functioning as lawmakers, publicists, teachers, psychologists, or even ad-

vertising managers, it is passing from those who were at least aware of
what value judgments they were making to those who are not; passing
into the hands of men who act on very inclusive and fateful judgments
while believing that they are acting on self-evident principles immune to
criticism. They do not know what they are making us into and refuse to
permit us even to ask.

Ellul sees the emerging technological society as "the pinnacle of
human submission," a world in which "children are educated to
become precisely what society expects of them." For a long time
shallow-thinking commencement speakers have been talking about
graduates "taking their place in society." Seldom, I am sure, have
these same speakers thought through the implications of their
cliche. Jacques Maritain says, "The essence of education does not
consist in adapting a potential citizen to the conditions and in-
teractions of social life, but first in *making a man,* and by this very
fact in preparing a citizen." In many instances guidance counselors
and school psychologists, trained in behaviorism's rat mazes, would
not agree. For them the dystopia of Michael Young's satire, *The
Rise of the Meritocracy,* is closer than some psychometricians and
social manipulators ever dreamed possible. C. S. Lewis predicted
that "the man-molders of the new age will be armed with the powers
of an omnicompetent state and an irresistible scientific technique:
we shall get at last a race of conditioners who really can cut out all
posterity in whatever shape they please."

It should be clear to anyone close to American public schools that
the technological state intends to eliminate the human teacher. He
will be replaced by a machine in as many instances as practicable,
as soon as possible. So says the most influential of the behavioral
psychologists, B. F. Skinner: "You can teach much more effectively
with devices of one kind or another. In the future they will be
commonplace in all instructional situations."

Although the arguments offered in favor of Skinner's "teaching
machines" are often related to dollars, the primary reason advocated is not merely financial. It is, instead, "educational accountability," a piece of jargon that measures the degree to which a
teacher—human or mechanical—can bring the class to a prescribed
level of accomplishment, following a prescribed program of study.
The measurement is calculated in terms of "behavioral change."
Teachers, according to the views of the National Educational

Technology Conference, are "managers of change." Pupils of these "managers" are now to be referred to as "clients."

"That's all teaching is," Skinner says, "arranging contingencies which bring about changes in behavior." In arithmetic, for example, a primary class begins without being able to compute by subtraction; subtraction is not one of the behaviors experienced by these children. *Accountability* could mean that 80 per cent of a given class has mastered simple subtraction to a level of 90 per cent accuracy on a given test by a prescribed date. In a junior high health education course, accountability might measure the class's ability to identify eight out of ten early-warning symptoms of cancer. In both cases, behavior would have changed. Aristotle would have called it "passing from ignorance to knowledge."

Presumably a human teacher could help this class achieve these "behavioral changes," although Skinner suggests otherwise. "The contingencies arranged without instrumental aid," he says with typical pleasure in jargon as a mode of discourse, "are often quite defective." In other words, the human teacher possesses dangerous liabilities as far as technology is concerned. He has his own opinions; he is also capable of veering from the approved syllabus. Not so the obedient computer. It is never sick or late or preoccupied with personal problems. It is steady, reliable, and therefore efficient. The machine performs faithfully at the level of efficiency demanded. It is therefore judged to be superior to the human teacher. In his newest book, *Beyond Freedom and Dignity,* Skinner boldly declares, "To man *qua* man we readily say good riddance." Here is that "abolition of man" against which Lewis warned.

In school districts throughout America, industrial corporations who have adopted Skinnerian methods in their technology are contracting to prove that their machine methods can produce faster and better results than human teachers have achieved. Their first subject areas are reading and mathematics. Westinghouse, RCA, Singer/Graflex, and Behavioral Research Laboratories are just a few of the companies involved. Usually their contracts have been for periods of three years, the companies to receive an incentive bonus after the first two years' tests are complete. The methods employed in the earliest instances have called down serious doubts about such industrial ethics as company representatives bribing "clients" with incentives of their own to encourage higher performances. In one notorious instance, in Texarkana, Arkansas, the contractor actually supplied answers in advance of the final test to improve over-all performances.

Where purveyors of "systems analysis" and "performance contracting" still share instructional responsibility, one of the favorite terms is "teacher-proof." The machine cannot be tampered with by the classroom teacher; therefore, the pupil's learning process cannot be interfered with. Roszak ironically describes this priority given to the teaching machine:

> If we discover that computers cannot teach as teaching at its most ideal is done, then we redesign education so that the machine can qualify as a teacher. . . . In this way man is replaced in all areas by the machine, not because the machine can do things "better," but rather because all things have been reduced to what the machine is capable of doing.

The argument here is not against so-called progress; it is not even against "teaching machines" as such. These gadgets are only objects of metal and plastic, subject to power failures and mechanical breakdown; they are only what some of their own advocates recognize as "expensive hardware configurations." Rather, what must be opposed is the *attitude* behind the use of machines to teach. This attitude contends that the human spirit can be comprehended by an inanimate manufactured implement, by "hardware" or "software." The assumption behind such an attitude is that man, as a mechanical entity responding to nervous stimuli, may be observed, tested, and programmed for his ability to cope with those stimuli. As such, man becomes a wholly predictable being. The educational manager can learn to recognize the proper stimuli, package them, and administer the program with assurance of results that will fall within pre-established norms. This is the new education.

As far as Skinner and his ilk are concerned, man is himself only a machine, scarcely as complex as some he has created. Yet according to one advertisement for technological learning methods, teaching machines themselves are "only the smallest tip of the iceberg." Precisely so, and it is the rest of that iceberg, still submerged in the imaginations of technological Gradgrinds, that threatens to wreck American schoolchildren.

Hildegard Hilton, writing in the *Connecticut English Journal,* reports on an editorial in an educational products catalog. It complains that among "impediments to objective evaluation of products" is "the teaching profession's concern for children rather than things." Can this be so? American education, especially at the highest echelons of state and federal policy making, is very close to making an unholy pact with industry that will turn the schools over to the technocrats. When this occurs, the new aims for education will simply parallel the old aims for the assembly line—a higher level of performance. Not better people but better products. As Ellul puts it, "According to this conception, education no longer has a humanist end or any value in itself; it has only one goal, to create technicians."

Any society that so dehumanizes its children presides over its own deathwatch. For if this depersonalization of education continues, we shall find ourselves without answers to Paul Goodman's questions in *Growing Up Absurd:*

> Who then will watch the puzzlement on a child's face and suddenly guess what it is that he *really* doesn't understand, that has apparently nothing to do with the present problem, nor even the present subject matter? and who will notice the light in his eyes and seize the opportunity to spread glorious clarity over the whole range of knowledge; for instance, the nature of succession and series, or what grammar really *is;* the insightful moments that are worth years of ordinary teaching.

No wonder, then, that our youth rebel, that the interdiction on an IBM card—"Do not fold, spindle, or mutilate"—has become a slogan for a generation that sees itself, again in Ellul's words, "smoothed out, like a pair of pants under a steam iron." No wonder our artists have almost despaired of creating the Beautiful, leaving us instead, as William Barrett says, with an image of man that is "riddled with gaps and holes, starkly finite." No wonder so many suffer from what Erich Fromm calls "moral aloneness."

In such a moral environment, the Christian school has a challenge and a responsibility unparalleled in its history because of its inherent stress upon the worth of each person as a creature of God. With men questioning their very dignity as human beings, the Christian school must assert its counter claims. The day may not be far off when the fact that the Christian school does *not* have automated teaching machines, does *not* specialize in turning classrooms into rat mazes—when this fact helps to define the purpose and philosophy of such a school.

The scoffer will charge (as did one representative of a manufacturer of classroom paraphernalia, when told that Stony Brook still preferred people to products) that such a decision is an instance of poor-mouthing. Anyone who can't afford to buy the latest gadgets, the scoffer will add, can scarcely have the temerity to criticize them.

But critize them, oppose them, accuse them of being what they are, the Christian school must. For the tools and methods of the new technocratic education are something far different from conveniences; they are not in a class with photocopiers, overhead projectors, videotape recorders, or cassette listening posts. Instead, some of the devices and their methods of application proposed by psychologists and manufactured by eager entrepreneurs impose the most narrowing and suffocating limitations on the human mind, the human spirit.

The result of technocracy's reduction of man to a cybernetic cipher will be, in Stanley Burnshaw's terms, "to break through the seamless web" of our wholeness as physical, emotional, intellectual and spiritual beings. When that happens, Burnshaw contends, man will have experienced the loss of Eden all over again. He will know, to his sorrow, the loss of "the primary pattern of human awareness and consciousness: the unitary condition of the species—man in a seamless web of relationships."

It is this web of relationships—what a girl newly arrived at Stony Brook calls "this incredible demonstration of love that I feel here"—that marks the Christian school as long as it continues its heritage: the well-trained, loving teacher caring for the body, mind, and soul of his pupil. This fact will before long distinguish the Christian school from its dehumanizing counterparts; it will also turn the Christian school into a place of refuge for parents who wish to retain the personhood of their children.

Yet in spite of these warnings, there are those who continue to look to secular education as the panacea. Gilbert Highet notes that "The young often feel lonely and lost. Good teaching helps them to feel they are part of the larger world." Perhaps so, unless the "good teaching" has been defined by a behavioral scientist as consisting of the warm companionship of a digital computer. Perhaps also, if the "good teaching" carries with it the advantages of truth. But *truth* is a mercurial word in education today. The famous institution whose motto is *Veritas* hesitates to declare what the motto means. Equivocation, hedging, and semantic circumlocutions protect the cynics in education: They neither know the truth themselves nor believe that anyone else can know it.

To the believing Christian, this cynicism seems perverse and demonic. Jesus Christ made perfectly clear his claim, "I am . . . the Truth." Yet for all its certainty in knowing Christ who is Truth, contemporary Christianity, especially that which calls itself evangelical, has not been successful in influencing the public education of young people. The Church, for the most part, has handed over the responsibility for education to the State, congratulating itself on its reasonable acceptance of the Constitution's proscription against any linkage of Church with State.

The Church has no right to congratulate itself. The Church has reneged on its apostolic mission to teach. The New Testament says nothing that would limit teaching to an hour in Sunday School once each week! Moreover, some branches of the Church have allowed the spawning of attitudes toward education that are apathetic at best, anti-intellectual at worst. Many Christian parents prefer to complain about the quality of public education rather than do something about it—either to take a personal part in local school's activities or else to seek out a Christian alternative. The Christian parent who is genuinely concerned about his children's public education can run for school board election, support another qualified candidate, or at least attend the public meetings and speak his convictions; he can support agencies such as the Religious Instruction Association, which helps public school teachers find legal methods of teaching the Bible in public schools; he can volunteer his own services and Christian influence in the many paraprofessional opportunities being offered today.

Remarkably enough, however, the same apparent apathy toward public education also carries over in the Church's attitude toward Christian education. Most churchgoing people do not seem to know the purposes and value of Christian schooling; nor do they seem to care. It cannot be that the Church is too impoverished financially to be able to afford the luxury of Christian education. Even evangelicalism has long since moved up from economic privation, as may be observed by checking the make and model of cars in church parking lots; another clue is the numerous advertisements for overseas tours appearing in evangelical magazines. While the evangelical church member has been prospering, however, most of these schools and colleges committed to training young men and women in Christian character languish for lack of funds.

John Blanchard, Jr., National Association of Christian Schools' executive director, says, "Christian private education must have financial support far beyond anything we have enjoyed in the past. A failure to recognize the role of the Christian school in our changing social scene will lead to our society's destruction as surely as the destruction of the dinosaurs."

Donn Gaebelein, addressing his faculty at the beginning of Stony Brook's fiftieth year, told them simply, "As you know, Stony Brook operates without any endowment to speak of. In this condition a school like ours is continually threatened."

Why are Christian schools not granted the measure of support due them from the American evangelical community? Perhaps the answer lies in the failure of the Christian school movement to define itself so clearly and to articulate its philosophy so fully as to compel the support of thoughtful Christians throughout the country. Edwin A. Rian summed up the disgrace of Christian education, saying, "The real plight of Protestant education is shockingly evident."

> These Protestant-related schools, for the most part, have no real philosophy of education, and practically no textbooks. Protestant schools as they exist today present no unified, integrated or formidable answer to the challenge of secularism. The plight of Protestant education is real and tragic.

A quarter-century has passed since Rian gave his indictment, but little has changed in Christian education as a whole. The evangelical Church remains, for the most part, indifferent to its responsibilities, unenlightened by a timid Christian pedagogy. "A little sleep, a little slumber, a little folding of the hands" describes the typical Christian attitude. Apart from some daring new methods employed by evangelistic organizations such as Campus Crusade,

Campus Life, and Inter-Varsity Christian Fellowship, far too little real progress has been made within the Church to define and implement a philosophy of Christian education. Even less has been done to create a philosophy that works in schools and colleges on a daily basis, although two notable exceptions are a curriculum study at Calvin College and some publications from Trinity Christian College.

Perhaps one of the reasons for the failure among Christian educators to create dynamic statements of their purposes and objectives lies in a basic attitude within evangelicalism. This attitude expresses itself in a denigration of theorizing. The very phrase, "Christian education," presupposes a conscious choice on the part of schoolmasters and their pupils (or their parents) to offer and receive an education that is uniquely Christian. Such a choice must begin with theory—with a deep searching out of the answers to ultimate questions such as "What is knowledge? How do we know? How can we tell if what we know is true?"; with the careful examination of educational objectives, methods, and alternatives; with an equally careful evaluation of the effects of the education experience. After such theorizing comes practice.

Too often Christian education operates in reverse. Action creates reaction, then evaluation occurs. Quiet contemplation is too expensive a luxury in an atmosphere of constant bustle—everyone busy serving the Lord. In some schools, shorthanded by financial difficulties, the pragmatic can-do teacher seems more useful than the philosophical theorist.

Yet is is wrong to assign the value of any Christian teacher on the basis of *either/or*—either the man of action or the man of reflection. Instead Christian education needs a *both/and* approach—*both* the philosophical study of Christian education with its difficult questions *and* a practical testing of the applications derived from that study. This duality ought to be part of the equipment of every teacher who presumes to serve in the Christian school.

In too many instances so-called Christian education is only Christian in piecemeal fashion. There has been too little serious thought given to the molding of a dynamic Christian curriculum. There has been too little attempt at creating, from any theoretical base, a truly Christian philosophy of education. Calvin Seerveld, professor of philosophy at Trinity Christian College, describes the problem and its solution this way:

> Christian education is not a matter of getting together a group of teachers somewhere till you have a simple majority of confessing Christians, each able to let his little evangelical light shine, and let it go at that, because Christian education takes in more than human endeavor. It takes place when the presence of the Lord is felt, known, seen, evident in the studying, wrestled and prayed for *communally* by the faculty, administrators, the board as one man on its knees, the parents behind it, the students too if you are blessed.

Perhaps contemporary Christians who desire a wholly Christian education should look to the example of an earlier group of Christian educators, men of the European Renaissance who practiced "Christian humanism."

                              *   *   *

The expression "Christian humanism" requires close defining, for like so many epithets, it has a tendency to slip into casual usage and lose its distinctives. Speaking on this same point in regard to Erasmus, Craig R. Thompson writes:

> If by "Christian humanism" we mean the interaction between classical culture and Christianity in the thought and work of Erasmus and like-minded men, the phrase makes sense. The trouble is that nowadays "humanism" is used by writers on ethics and religion as a counter to "supernaturalism" or "theism." . . . If "Christian" and "humanist" are antithetical terms, then to call Erasmus or anybody else a Christian humanist is nonsense, and chaos is come again.

Erasmus himself, in a passage quoted on page 70, gives the simplest and most effective definition of Christian humanism available or necessary. He speaks of the teacher whose two concerns are "the best literature" and "the love of Christ." Humanism was a development of the Renaissance—one could argue that humanism was a "rebirth" in itself—characterized ¡by a newly awakened appreciation for the Greek and Roman classics. Prior to the rise of humanism in the early fifteenth century, European thought had been controlled by scholasticism, a medieval obscurantism that ignored pagan classical art. The scholastic mind was closed to that which did not bear the hallmark of Christian orthodoxy although somehow the logic and metaphysics of Aristotle remained acceptable.

A bridge between medieval scholasticism and Renaissance humanism was formed by the creation of Dante's *Divine Comedy,* written between 1307 and 1321. Here, for the first time in any successful manner, the artist brought together the substantive truth of Greek and Roman myth with the revealed truth of Scripture. The result created an unsurpassed imaginative description of iniquity, judgment, restoration, and divine sublimity. *The Divine Comedy* stands as the nonpareil of literature.

Like Dante, many artists and scholars of the next three centuries were believing Christians. They gave themselves to *studià humanitatis*—that is, to the study of literature, philosophy, history, and the fine arts. They found in their attraction to the humanities no contradiction of their love for God and reverence for the Scriptures. On the contrary, they recognized that the best artists and writers confirmed in their work what the Scriptures teach about the nature of man. In so doing, of course, they controverted the famous dictum of Tertullian, "What indeed has Athens to do with Jerusalem?"

Furthermore, as Douglas Bush shows in *The Renaissance and English Humanism,* the purpose of all learning was to amplify one's capacity to glorify God. He quotes Erasmus, who said, "All studies, philosophy, rhetoric are followed for this one object, that we may know Christ and honor Him. This is the end of all learning and eloquence."

The designation, "Christian humanism," is a noble one and carries with it some of the names of the greatest thinkers and doers in Western civilization. We have already mentioned the names of Vittorino da Feltre, the schoolmaster of Mantua; John Amos Comenius, called by Cotton Mather "that incomparable Moravian"; and Desiderius Erasmus, whose name is synonymous with scholarship. Others to be included, purely from the ranks of those whose art was verbal, range from Petrarch in Italy to Sir Thomas More in England to Blaise Pascal in France. Bush concludes the chain of literary artists with Milton, "the last great exponent of Christian humanism in its historical continuity." But he makes an addition worth noting: Shakespeare, whose "imaginative world is conditioned by the religious and ethical values of Christian humanism." Thus, the heritage of Christian humanism may be said to include the three primary poets since Homer—Dante, Shakespeare, and Milton—and still leave unmentioned the scholars, painters, sculptors, musicians, architects, and teachers of the humanities who shared in its development.

The modern writer scarcely need apologize for asserting the claims of Christian humanism except in recognition of his own meager claims to stand in that tradition. Yet stand in it he must, if as a Christian educator he wishes to defend the Holy City from the onslaught of the barbarians. Still, one must face the fact that "Christian humanism" will seem semantically indigestible to those who have been trained to understand "humanism" as a synonym for "atheism." One can hardly go around giving vocabulary lessons or short courses in cultural and intellectual history to all the people who might be offended by a juxtaposition of "Christian" and "humanist." Instead an alternative term must be found.

As a straightforward substitute, we need *Christian art and scholarship* practiced by *Christian artists and scholars.* Those who qualify will be recognizable through willingness to give witness to their personal faith in Jesus Christ as Lord; through their desire to use their art and intellect to communicate the love of God to the whole world; through their earnest efforts to follow the aesthetic and spiritual principles laid down in the Scriptures, particularly in St. Paul's admonition, "Whatever is true, . . . honorable, . . . just, . . . pure, . . . lovely, . . . think about these things." They will differ from artists and scholars who are not Christian in several respects, not the least of which is the worth accorded the human being as a potential child of God, reconciled to him by faith. The Christian artist, the Christian scholar, will have as his "unifying principle," to quote Frank Gaebelein, "the recognition that *all truth is God's truth.*" This will be his axiom. He will know, with Maritain, that "truth does not depend on us but on *what is.*" As for *what is,* the Christian will find that authoritatively stated in the Bible. This truth—the truth about God and man, time and eternity, redemption and judgment—he will take as his world-view, the promontory from which he looks out upon life.

The Christian artist, the Christian scholar, will have the same high objective expressed by Erasmus: "that we may know Christ and honor Him." Not even the Nobel Prize is more important than this. To achieve this high goal requires a passionate sense of purpose, not unlike that attributed to Ellul by his translator, John Wilkinson. Wilkinson calls Ellul "a Christian" and then proceeds to explain what this means:

> [Ellul's] concept of the duty of a Christian, who stands uniquely (is "present") at the point of intersection of this material world and the eternal world to come, is not to concoct ambiguous ethical schemes or programs of social action, but to testify to the truth of both worlds and thereby to affirm his freedom through the revolutionary nature of his religion.

If contemporary Christian artists and scholars are to have any effect at all upon society, it must be through a willingness to affirm, through the revolutionary nature of their faith, their freedom. The Christian faith is that which revolutionizes man's spirit and liberates him from the bondage of intolerance, greed, lust, pride, and selfishness. In schools where religious instruction is permitted, the Christian artist and scholar must assert forthrightly man's dignity and distinctiveness as God's special work of creation, even though fallen in sin. To do so in a manner that will withstand the vagaries of the future, Christians must develop new attitudes toward the role of artists and scholars as educators in a troubled society. It is time, as Lev Shestov has said, "to throw off the power of the soulless and entirely indifferent truths into which the fruits of the tree of knowledge have been transformed."

*   *   *

In the future, if Christian education is to develop as an effective force in American society, a new attitude must be defined regarding *power*. On the whole evangelical Christians have been unusually naive about power, in spite of their habit of quoting New Testament passages in which power is promised. "Ye shall receive power," said the resurrected Jesus; the Gospel of Christ is "the power of God unto salvation," wrote the Apostle Paul. But few Christians have been willing to go beyond these spiritual applications of power to find another description. This description of power relates to man's sense of authority; it is fundamental to man's sense of himself.

The Greek philosopher of the fifth century before Christ,

Protagoras, thought he knew the source and substance of power. In a treatise of which only the first line survives, he wrote, "Man is the measure of all things." Over 2500 years later, just as the armies of the Third Reich and Imperial Japan were sweeping their way across whole continents, Erich Fromm chose to echo Protagoras' maxim. In a strange refusal to consider current events, Fromm declared that "man is all by himself, . . . there is no authority which gives meaning to life except man himself."

These assertions of man's primacy are being contradicted on every hand, as we have been suggesting, by the new technocracy. The Sophists of fifth century Greece have been co-opted in John Kenneth Galbraith's "new industrial state." The Christian who loves God and reveres the revelation of truth in nature, art, and science stands between man and his destruction by dehumanizing processes. Such a Christian was Blaise Pascal, whose *Pensees* testify to his faith. Pascal knew man better than Fromm does and wrote, "Man is but a reed, the most feeble thing in nature, but he is a thinking reed . . . he knows that he dies." Two centuries later William Hazlitt wrote, "Man is the only animal that laughs and weeps; for he is the only animal that is struck with the difference between what things are, and what they ought to be."

These estimates of man and his paltry condition are closer to the truth than Protagoras' claim. In the universe at large, man is powerless, especially if robbed of his relationship to a divine Creator. Then, as Bacon said, "if he be not of kin to God by his spirit, he is a base and ignoble creature." But power among men exists, and from that power an authority is derived which must be used for good; else, it will be used to pervert the good.

If Christian education is to be effective, it must learn how to use three important authorities at hand. First, it must make a renewed assertion of the propositional truths of the Bible. The Gospel is "the power of God unto salvation," though the Gospel is not confined to the page alone. It is also present in nature: "The heavens declare the glory of God." It is present in history: "Lo, all these things worketh God oftentimes with man." It is supremely present in the Person of Jesus Christ: "I came that they might have life, and have it abundantly." It is present in the Church, in the sacraments, in the personal experience of witnessing believers. But the Gospel obtains its authority in these other manifestations from their corroboration of the written record. If the Bible had claimed that one condition were true and history showed a different condition, the contradiction of observed fact would invalidate the apparent authority. But such is not the case.

Too often Christian education as it presently exists has taken a timid view of its commitment to the authority of the Bible. There were times at Stony Brook, for example, when the Bible courses were not taught with sufficient academic rigor. In the hands of some sincere but inadequate teachers, the Bible course deteriorated to something barely above the level of a Sunday School class. The Christian school must not allow the teaching of its principal text to be below the quality of its teaching in other classes. In every Christian school the study of the Bible must be done with academic integrity and in a manner that accounts both for the simplicity of its message and the profundity of its truth. The authority of the Bible as the central revelation of truth to Christian artists and scholars as educators must never be diminished by human failure to give the Bible the highest place in personal study and devotion.

Next to an open assertion of biblical authority, the Christian school must claim the authority of personal example. This subject, already dealt with at some length in Chapter Four, nonetheless needs re-emphasis here. Edmund Burke said, "Example is the school of mankind, and they will learn at no other." In the classroom who the teacher is may well be more important than what the subject is, for the testimony of long experience shows that when textbooks and authors, theories and formulas, have been forgotten, the name of the teacher remains inbedded in memory. With the name lodges the example.

Bishop Fulton J. Sheen has written, "If one is teaching science or mathematics, even history or literature, the main thing is to be lucid. But for the teaching of ideas which could call upon a man to change his life, lucidity is not enough. The self of the teacher has to make contact with the self of the hearer." But when the self of the teacher and the personal example of character are lifted from the classroom, replaced by a blinking light and a scanning screen (as Skinner's successors promise will be so), the pupil loses the principal impetus among children for learning, namely, the emulation of a good and wise teacher. Of course, where the example is bad, where the teacher is unwholesome or incompetent, grave damage may be done. But I speak here of the Christian teacher, the artist and scholar whose own example is Jesus himself.

In the character of such teachers the Christian school ought to find a new power, a new sense of authority—not an authority such as led Comenius to describe the schools of his day as "grinding houses," nor an authority that imposes piousness like a dress regulation, but the authority that derives from spiritual principles put into daily practice. In this matter of setting an example, the Christian school may rightly expect that support of parents. Again, the wisdom of Comenius is worth noting:

> Let not parents, therefore, devolve the whole instruction of their children upon teachers of schools and ministers of the church. It is impossible to make a tree straight that has grown crooked, or produce an orchard from a forest everywhere surrounded with briers and thorns.

The example of the home must complement that of the school if the child is to receive the full benefits of Christian nurture.

There is a third authority upon which the Christian school can draw, once it has established the other two. That is the authority of its own tradition and contribution. The Christian school, made up of artists and scholars who are dedicated to knowing Christ and honoring him, has a strength which it can rightly claim. It has principles of which it can be justly proud. It participates in the grandest tradition in Western civilization. As such, the Christian school can anticipate its own contribution to the immediate community. It has much to contribute.

The apologetic expressions on the faces of some so-called Christian teachers and administrators leaves one wondering if they know the majesty of their calling. Read again Erasmus: "It is the noblest of occupations."

Christian education, as described by St. Paul to the Corinthians, does not depend upon "the wisdom of the wise" or "the cleverness of the clever." But the teaching given by Paul is simply "Christ the power of God and the wisdom of God." Christians today must claim again this power and this wisdom. Joseph Haroutunian urges:

> If a school calls itself Christian and if the faculty of such a school believe in Christ as the wisdom and power of God, yea, in the cross as the

redemption of man and therewith of the total life of man, then I do not see how it can escape its responsibility, its most grave responsibility, to God, man and country, for making its own indispensable contribution to the total educational enterprise.

To make such a contribution, the Christian school will have to follow its assertion of power with a new attitude toward *time*. In particular, the Christian school must reset its clocks to conform to a new awareness of eschatological time. Twenty years ago Frank Gaebelein spoke of "the rediscovery of eschatology" and summoned Christian education to "be about its business, not held back but spurred on by the urgency of the times."

Today the Church may not be any more aware of the imminent return of Christ than it was two decades ago, but many on the fringe or outside the structure of the Church are declaring their belief in Doomsday. The August 1971 issue of *Ramparts* magazine reports on "the Jesus freaks" and the writer says,

> But over-arching all else is a passionate belief that the world will end within their lifetime while Jesus returns to rapture them off to a very literal heaven with streets of gold and angels twanging on electric-amp harps.

When scoffers and skeptics can recognize the paramount importance of the Second Coming to Christian doctrine, it would seem strange not to find the same realization in schools calling themselves Christian.

How should a Christian school demonstrate its alertness to Last Things? To deal first with the extreme, the doctrine of the return of Christ in no way precludes the Christian institution from pursuing its responsibilities on a long-range basis. Its building and development programs must be conducted with an eye to the future. At the same time the heart of the enterprise must not be with the buildings and the equipment themselves. In the very act of their dedication to service for God, the Christian educator must understand that all his tools are marked with a projected obsolescence. There is a date after which he will need them no longer. Until then, however, he must work like a diligent steward in obedience to Christ, who said, "Occupy till I come."

Such a sense of time ought to free the Christian school from the frenzy of being schedule-bound and frustrated by its apparent failures in the immediate. The nervous fascination with *now*—the jerky, impulsive abandoning of one program for a newer, merely more contemporary program—the collapse of good will among students and faculty over some temporary setback—the foolish reluctance of an adult to recognize the truth of what Erasmus said, "Remember, that your pupil is a boy still, and that you were a boy yourself not so long ago"—these are common hindrances within Christian schools, where one might reasonably expect to find a greater understanding of "the fullness of time" and of Providential concern about the affairs of men both in time and in eternity.

A Christian school cannot usurp the role of God and tamper with God's timing. When its students seem most calloused toward the message of the Gospel, the Christian school cannot, by any means within its own power, eliminate the present antagonism. What the school can do—what it must do—is to continue its ministry in total fidelity to its Christian purpose, allowing God who is the very Author of time to work out all things according to his divine will. This is the proper stewardship of time.

The manner in which the school expresses itself in regard to the future will be a clue to its sense of eschatological time. In accord with New Testament principles, the Christian school must live with the serenity of a known future. Exigencies common to all schools will come and go; the school's sense of ongoing purpose remains. Whereas the secular-minded school looks in distress at unforeseen contingencies, the Christian school regards the consummation of the Ages as its ultimate Commencement.

Such an attitude must be reflected in the school's teaching. Haroutunian has said:

> There is nothing more incongruous and defeating in a Christian school than that the sciences, and especially the humanities, should be taught as though man's last business were not with God.

This does not mean that one distorts science or literature or history to serve merely as sermon topics in the classroom. But it does mean, as Haroutunian pointed out, that there is such a thing as a Christian understanding of *Hamlet* and *Moby Dick*, of Mozart and Cezanne; of Adam Smith and Karl Marx; of Greek history and American politics; of anxiety and social disintegration.

The Christian world-view, encompassing all knowledge within the framework of God's truth, does not admit of compromise. There is no such thing as part-time Christian education. One cannot decide, as an English teacher for example, to stress the evident implications of Christian truth in *King Lear* or *A Farewell to Arms* and not insist upon the same standard of truth in the teaching of rhetoric or grammar. The fact that these implications may be somewhat more difficult for the teacher to discern is no indication that they are not present and require exposition. Too often the failure of professing Christian teachers to find the integration of truth and their discipline results from their inadequate grasp of the subject. Better scholarship produces better saints.

In total candor, it must be said that when a Christian teacher does not represent the whole truth about his subject, including its implicit spiritual ramifications, he is guilty of a serious omission. To the degree that he stands aside from what he knows to be a fuller description of truth, the Christian teacher has diminished his students' apperception of truth.

Obviously a great number of public school teachers who are also believing Christians stand in a jeopardized position. As teachers in a pluralistic state, they are forbidden to use their classrooms as religious forums. It is to be hoped, however, that the Christian who teaches in tax-supported public institutions redeems every other opportunity to complete his witness.

T.S. Eliot's warning, from a pub-keeper in *The Waste Land,* is also a challenge: "HURRY UP PLEASE ITS TIME." The Christian school, its artists and scholars, and those who are its constituents must respond with a clearer sense of mission in eschatological terms.

This mission will find its expression in the Christian school's *curriculum* and its relevance for the future. I do not use "relevance" in any slangy fashion; I do not mean that the Christian school should "get with it." I mean that if Christian artists and scholars on its faculty intend to speak and be heard, they must speak on the issues that are most urgent. "Most urgent," however, may not necessarily coincide with "most interesting," at least not at the outset. A current handbook for teachers bears as its telling title *Teach Us What We Want to Know*. There is often a significant difference, unfortunately, between what children and young people *want* to know and what they *need* to know. The curriculum of the Christian school must meet its students' needs. In this fundamental point lies the greatest distinction between current secular education, geared for the pupil's wishes, and Christian education, geared for the glory of God. Experience has shown, however, that in their presentation by a skillful teacher, the ultimate issues are never dull. To young people motivated to serious thought for the first time, the paramount concerns become more than merely interesting.

What are the most urgent issues for a Christian curriculum? They may be summed up by the great Christian commandment: "You shall love the Lord your God with all your heart, and with all your soul, and with all your strength, and with all your mind; and your neighbor as yourself." To love the Lord God is more than a spiritual act; to love one's neighbor is more than an emotional gesture; to love and respect oneself is more than a psychological necessity. These are also to be expressed through our minds, through a conscious appreciation of the grandeur of God and the relationship we experience with Him and others.

It is no cheap formula to say that love for God may be stimulated through the study of mathematics and science as descriptions of the universe He has created. Love for neighbor may be engendered by a study of world history, anthropology, geography, the languages and cultures of other people. Love and respect for self, which Jesus tied to love for others, may be developed through an appreciation for the total human being; it may also result from the study of literature, national history, and art; it should come from a growing desire to express oneself in language and in other forms of communication.

The study of mathematics and science must be redirected away from mere vocational training. One does not study physics to become a physicist, Maritain contends, but to *know* physics. The Christian teacher of these disciplines must present them in their ultimate value as methods for classifying and measuring the wonders of God's creation. A closer relationship must be drawn between geometry and art, between mathematics and music, between physics and language. Perhaps a useful starting point, as a strategy for eliminating a utilitarian attitude toward learning, would be to mix various classifications of knowledge: to speak of Euclidean *rhetoric* or the *grammar* of chemistry or the *constituent analysis* of a problem in history.

In reaffirming the tradition of Christian humanism, it is natural that a high place be given to the humanities. But this must become the pattern in every Christian school. The study of history, literature, and rhetoric; opportunities for creativity in drama, music, art, and writing; learning and using ancient and modern languages, especially outside the sterility of a "language lab"; obtaining a grasp on the political system and on civic responsiblities—these must flourish along with the study of God's Word in the Christian school.

The most neglected areas of education in Christian schools have been those pertaining to health and physical education. These would seem obligatory in a school that claims the indwelling of God in the bodies of men. Athletic programs are not enough. Team sports teach co-operation and a sense of selflessness, but coaches rarely have time to instruct their athletes in the marvel of creation that is the human body. Courses in health education, including responsible instruction in sexual development and mental health, are properly integral with biblical teaching that the body is the temple of the Holy Spirit. The Christian school must also instruct its pupils, as St. Paul told young Timothy, that "bodily training is of some value," and point to the necessity of caring for the body throughout life.

In his book *The Gospel and Christian Education,* D. Campbell Wyckoff writes,

> Christian education takes place as God's will, the church's purposes, the teacher's goals, and the pupils aims are acknowledged, weighed, and blended. The first and major classroom task is the reconciliation of all these objectives, and the planning of classroom activities in the light of the result.

Each school will find its own best way to implement such a curriculum. Presumably the school of the future will be far less sedentary than today's classrooms. More learning experiences will be offered in the community where a local site or museum offers an opportunity for first-hand study of history, where a geological formation or a botanical peculiarity makes analysis possible, where a community art show or amateur theater provides opportunities for the development of taste and critical perception.

The curriculum of the Christian school must instill in its students a respect for the past; it must prepare them for the future. But it cannot afford to ignore its responsibilities in the present. Christianity for too long has given its energies to past and future, earning from some critics an accusation of being an obscurantist religion. To be relevant means to be pertinent to the times. The present struggles in American society will continue to be upon us, no doubt in greater intensity, in the years ahead. The Christian school must bring upon these conflicts the light of its biblical perspective.

Issues such as citizenship, poverty, race, and war must be discussed with openness. Current events, about which so many Americans seem oblivious, must not be treated lightly by the Christian educator. The Twenty-sixth Amendment now enfranchises the 18-year-old. What will be his political philosophy? The Christian school must accept the bulk of responsibility for enlightening each of its pupils to the political process. Here again, the wholly sedentary approach must be discarded. Students from every Christian school must converge on political assemblies—from town meetings to the Congress of the United States. They must meet local legislators, county executives, and town supervisors of highways and sewers. They must learn why traffic lights seem to take an inordinate length of time to be installed; they must come to understand why the selling of detergents has been banned in their county; they must know both sides of the welfare problem, the housing problem, the labor-management problem.

Jacques Maritain says, "The Christian mind has to cleanse itself of social prejudices due to historical sclerosis." The Christian school must take the lead in this cleansing and renewal so that the blood of Christ may flow freely to the regeneration of all men.

Wyckoff lists ten questions the answers to which are essential "in order to get the curriculum principles we need." One of his questions is "What organizing principle shall be used to guarantee the curriculum's unity?" In all the present discussion of curriculum the central place given to the study of the Bible, as previously discussed, is assumed. This one great advantage the Christian school may claim over its secular counterparts: the presence in the curriculum of a central focus. The educator Robert K. Hutchins has pointed out that in the secular mode of education, where "the crucial error is that of holding that nothing is any more important than anything else, . . . the course of study goes to pieces because there is nothing to hold it together." Such should not be true of the school that earnestly seeks to correlate its search for truth around the revelation of the Scriptures.

Only in this way can Christian education hope to end what Maritain calls "the cleavage between religious inspiration and secular activity in man." Only through the integration of the Word of God with the phenomena of meteorites, the Shakespearean sonnet, the gross national product, and irregular French verbs can education be redeemed, can man experience, in Maritain's terms, "sanctification of profane and secular existence."

For the Christian school to achieve success in its mission requires a new attitude toward *excellence.* In some quarters Alfred North Whitehead's call for "the pursuit of excellence" has become an academic bromide; in others, an impossible dream. Donn Gaebelein and Peter Haile were approached by the head of another Christian school at a conference on Christian education and asked, in all sincerity, "Don't you really think that Stony Brook's desire for excellence gets in the way of your Christian testimony?"

D. Elton Trueblood might have answered, "We must, as Christians, stress excellence. Holy shoddy is still shoddy." In the earliest years of The Stony Brook School, John F. Carson would challenge the board with these words: "We must not pass off a cheap education in the name of God." The school that contents itself with learning experiences that are admittedly less than that school's capabilities is a fraud and a blight on the name of Christ.

To an embarrassing degree some Christian schools have fostered a spirit of contentment with the second-rate as long as the spiritual attitude remains commendable. Such schools, James Kallas says, offer "a substitution of piety for intellectual effort." Well-meaning teachers encourage pseudo-Christian explications of literature (Penelope is the faithful Church waiting for the imminent return of Odysseus as emblematic of the Second Coming of Christ). The most superficial attack on the theory of evolution receives praise for its defense of biblical creationism. "In this system," Kallas notes, "one who can write 'I love Jesus' in a nicely flowing hand gets 'A' for English."

But, Joseph Haroutunian rightly insists, "Christian schools must educate better and not worse than secular schools." To do so requires a commitment to excellence from each administrator, teacher, and staff worker; it requires the daily practice of such a commitment. In pursuing excellence no aspect of the school's daily business or the individual teacher's behavior can be set aside as unrelated to the goal. No activity or gesture may be discounted. The school will be what the man is, and the man is known by his common traits.

If a campus or school building is littered, if its desks and walls are marred by graffiti, if its lawns are spoiled by short-cut paths, the visitor can quickly acquire a sense of the school and its attitude toward excellence. If a teacher is consistently late for his classes, if his lectures seem disorganized or uncertain, if his students must often wait a week or more to learn the results of an examination— these students may rightly call into question the seriousness of their teacher's sense of Christian vocation as well as his commitment to excellence.

To approach the excellence toward which it strives, the Christian school also requires the wholehearted dedication of its board of trustees and other officers. In the past some people seemed to feel that the chief function of a trustee in a Christian enterprise was to give powerful endorsement through the weight of his reputation. Today the Christian school needs much more: it needs men and women as trustees who are actively raising and investing funds for the support of the institution. Education today costs money, increasingly greater sums of money, to maintain conditions in which learning may occur. Finding and wisely spending this money is the responsibility of the trustees. Only those who believe in the mission of the school can afford to be its *trustees*—those to whom policy making and financial affairs have been entrusted.

At Stony Brook, Donn Gaebelein has been working with a board that seems willing to shape itself to fulfill its obligation as trustees. Of course the nature of the Stony Brook board has altered greatly since the difficult days after World War II. For one thing, the board of twenty-one members now includes thirteen alumni; three other members are fathers of alumni. Their interests are centered upon the School rather than divided by some adjunct to the ministry, as was true during the years of the Stony Brook Assembly. And Gaebelein has made it clear that he does not intend to do what, at times, his father had to do—drag the board to make decisions. "I'm sure," he says wryly, "that some of the old board members took for granted that God would honor my father's faith, so they sat back and prayed." Gaebelein has reminded the present board that Stony Brook is their school; it is before God that they hold the School in trust.

The Christian school must also receive the confidence and patience of parents willing to enroll their children and willing, whenever possible, to give their time to the active support of the school in many of its programs. The Christian school should derive its greatest strength not from the institutional church but from the Christian home. In turn, the Christian school should reinforce the virtues being taught in the Christian home and help bring them to fruition in the excellence of character.

Cardinal Newman regarded the object of education as "nothing more or less than intellectual excellence." This must be the Christian teacher's standard. To assist him in reaching this standard, the Christian teacher needs the wisdom and scholarship of leaders among Christian schools. In particular, the teacher needs teaching materials to use with his students to augment the witness of his own character. The Bible is his primary aid, but he also needs textbooks and other supplies to support his teaching.

For too long Christian teachers have had little other choice in textbooks than the standard texts published for the public schools. These books often conflict with aspects of the Christian faith or with elements of religious history. Directly, a history textbook may present an incomplete portrait of an important Christian—Luther or Calvin, for instance—thereby leaving an unqualifiedly negative opinion. Indirectly, a literature anthology can distort the values of art or give an essentially untrue description of a writer's thought merely through its biased table of contents; interpretive introductions and study apparatus in textbooks may also be slanted in subtle ways antagonistic to a Christian view of the discipline. These same observations may be made about many films, filmstrips, and other audio-visual materials manufactured for public distribution. Criticism of this kind presumes, of course, that the Christian teacher has already acquired a Christian view of his vocation and of his subject. To counter these negative influences, the Christian teacher has needed to create many of his own materials; he has also needed to keep reminding his pupils of the textbook's fallibility—itself a difficult task for any classroom teacher when what *the book says* differs from the truth as he knows it!

Such attempts at preparing one's own teaching materials, however, usually end in frustration and failure. Few teachers are imaginative enough or have the resources of time and money to be able to produce lesson guides and illustrations to rival those of the major publishers. Too often what the pupils receive is a smudged mineographed leaflet prepared under pressure and lacking the visual appeal of a standard textbook. The Christian school movement desperately needs the publishing of first-rate textbooks in all subjects, at all grade levels, to complement the teacher's own creativity.

For the encouragement of all Christian teachers, the publication of *Biology: A Search for Order in Complexity* by the Zondervan Publishing House (1970) may be the ushering in of a new age. Prepared by the textbook committee of the Creation Research Society, a group of distinguished Christian scholars, this biology textbook compares favorably with any secular book: its illustrations are attractive, its type is highly readable; it has nothing of a cheap appearance to it. Moreover, it is an honest book, for it states outrightly in its preface what its position is concerning creation and the theory of evolution:

> Evidence for evolution as a *theory* of origins are accurately presented and considered. At the same time, it is explicit throughout the text that the most reasonable explanation for the actual facts of biology as they are known scientifically is that of Biblical creationism.

The excellence of a publishing project such as this recommends a broadening into other fields of study. But Christian publishing companies cannot be asked to risk sums of money required for a textbook series without reasonably expecting the support of

Christian schools. The only reason that the major secular firms invest in Roman Catholic textbooks has been that they can be assured of a reliable market. The Christian school will never achieve its goal of integrating all learning into an experience of faith until it has demanded and obtained the best tools for the job.

Yet a warning is necessary to the Christian artist and scholar and to the Christian school following "the pursuit of excellence." The pitfall of intellectual pride awaits the haughty, as the Book of Proverbs warns. No teacher, whatever his religious profession, was ever truly successful if his pedagogy became mere pedantry, a show of his superior knowledge. H. L. Mencken advised that the best teacher is "one who is essentially childlike." Certainly it is not the man who knows much who is the excellent teacher but the man who knows how to express what he knows so that others may learn it. A wise schoolmaster put the matter more pointedly when he told his faculty, "Remember, gentlemen, when you enter your classes that you are in the presence of your academic superiors."

Haroutunian suggests that "one contribution of Christian teaching . . . should be an adequate understanding of humility." He presses his argument against the teacher and says, "A teacher who lectures all the time is not likely to be a humble man no matter how he feels." And Comenius gives an added warning when he declares, "God does not call us to heaven asking us smart questions. It is more profitable to know things humbly than to know them proudly."

In one of the truly profound statements about education, Alfred North Whitehead says, "Moral education is impossible apart from the habitual vision of greatness." Unfortunately, Whitehead's definition of *greatness,* in the context of his remark, rises no higher than the classical literature of Greece and Rome. The Christian artist and scholar, the Christian school, knows a higher source.

On the pulpit in Hegeman Memorial Chapel at Stony Brook, this inscription faces the speaker: "Sir, we would see Jesus." This must be the habitual vision placed before each student by the Christian teacher. Examples of purposeful living and estimable character are inadequate of themselves unless they point to the source of true excellence, in the Person of Jesus Christ the Lord.

A Selected Bibliography

Education: History, Philosophies, and Methods

Barr, Donald. *Who Pushed Humpty Dumpty?* New York: Atheneum, 1971.

Bloom, Benjamin S., *et al. Taxonomy of Education Objectives.* New York: McKay, 1956 (Vol. I) and 1964 (Vol. II).

Conant, James B. *Education and Liberty.* Cambridge: Harvard University Press, 1953.

Dewey, John. *Experience and Education.* New York: Macmillan, 1938.

Dworkin, Martin S. (ed.). *Dewey on Education.* New York: Bureau of Publications, Teachers College, Columbia University, 1959.

Ellul, Jacques. *The Technological Society.* New York: Knopf, 1964.

Evans, Richard I. *B. F. Skinner: The Man and His Ideas.* New York: Dutton, 1968.

Frankena, William K. *Three Historical Philosophies of Education.* Chicago: Scott, Foresman, 1965.

Goodman, Paul. *Growing Up Absurd.* New York: Random House, 1960.

Highet, Gilbert. *The Art of Teaching.* New York: Vintage, 1957.

Hutchins, Robert K. *Education for Freedom.* Baton Rouge: Louisiana State University Press, 1943.

Krutch, Joseph Wood. *The Measure of Man.* New York: Grosset and Dunlap, 1953.

Roszak, Theodore. *The Making of a Counter Culture.* Garden City: Doubleday, 1969.

Rushdoony, Rousas J. *The Messianic Character of American Education.* Nutley, N. J.: The Craig Press, 1968.

Rusk, Robert R. *The Philosophical Bases of Education.* Boston: Houghton Mifflin, 1956.

Silberman, Charles E. *Crisis in the Classroom.* New York: Random House, 1970.

Skinner, B.F. *Beyond Freedom and Dignity.* New York: Random House, 1971.

Whitehead, Alfred North. *The Aims of Education.* New York: New American Library, 1959.

Woodward, William Harrison. *Vittorino da Feltre and Other Humanist Educators.* New York: Bureau of Publications, Teachers College, Columbia University, 1964.

———. *Desiderius Erasmus concerning the Aim and Method of Education.* New York: Bureau of Publications, Teachers College, Columbia University, 1964.

Wynne, John P. *Theories of Education.* New York: Harper and Row, 1963.

Young, Michael. *The Rise of the Meritocracy: 1870-2033.* Baltimore, Md.: Penguin Books, 1968.

Christian Education

Calvin College Curriculum Study Committee. *Christian Liberal Arts Education.* Grand Rapids: Calvin College and Eerdmans, 1970.

Cogley, John. *Religion in a Secular Age: The Search for Final Meaning.* New York: Praeger, 1968.

Comenius, John Amos. *The School of Infancy* (ed. Will S. Monroe). Boston: Heath, 1896.

Cully, Kendig Brubaker. *The Search for a Christian Education— Since 1940.* Philadelphia: Westminster, 1965.

DeGraaf, Arnold. *The Educational Ministry of the Church: A Perspective.* Nutley, N. J.: The Craig Press, 1968.

Fuller, Edmund (ed.). *The Christian Idea of Education.* New Haven: Yale University Press, 1957.

Gaebelein, Frank E. *Christian Education in a Democracy.* New York: Oxford University Press, 1951.

———. *The Pattern of God's Truth.* New York: Oxford University Press, 1954.

———. *A Varied Harvest.* Grand Rapids: Eerdmans, 1967.

———, Earl G. Harrison, and William L. Swing. (eds.). *Education for Decision.* New York: Seabury, 1963.

Jaarsma, Cornelius. *Fundamentals in Christian Education: Theory and Practice.* Grand Rapids: Eerdmans, 1953.

Johnson, F. Ernest (ed.). *American Education and Religion.* New York: Harper, 1952.

Lewis, C.S. *The Abolition of Man.* New York: Macmillan, 1962.

Maritain, Jacques. *Education at the Crossroads.* New Haven: Yale University Press, 1943.

Moore, Peter C. (ed.). *Youth in Crisis.* New York: Seabury, 1966.

Panoch, James V. and David L. Barr. *Religion Goes to School: A Practical Handbook for Teachers.* New York: Harper and Row, 1968.

Rian, Edwin H. *Christianity and American Education.* San Antonio: The Naylor Company, 1949.

Rushdoony, Rousas J. *Intellectual Schizophrenia.* Philadelphia: Presbyterian and Reformed Publishing Company, 1961.

Sadler, John Edward. *J. A. Comenius and the Concept of Universal Education.* New York: Barnes and Noble, 1966.

Seerveld, Calvin. *Cultural Objectives for the Christian Teacher.* Palos Heights, Ill.: Trinity Christian College, no date.

Spinka, Matthew. *John Amos Comenius: That Incomparable Moravian.* New York: Russell and Russell, 1967.

Sweet, William Warren. *The Story of Religion in America.* New York: Harper, 1950.

Thorne, Charles G., Jr. *Word or Words. A View of Religion in Independent Schools.* Wallingford, Conn.: Council for Religion in Independent Schools, 1971.

von Grueningen, John Paul (ed.). *Toward a Christian Philosophy of Higher Education.* Philadelphia: Westminster, 1957.

Worrell, Edward K. *Restoring God to Education.* Wheaton, Ill.: Van Kampen Press, 1950.

Wyckoff, D. Campbell. *The Gosp3l and Christian Education.* Philadelphia: Westminster, 1959.

Zylstra, Henry. *Testament of Vision.* Grand Rapids: Eerdmans, 1958.

Independent Schools

Chamberlain, Ernest B. *Our Independent Schools.* New York: American Book Company, 1944.

Committee of the Faculties of Andover, Exeter, Lawrenceville, Harvard, Princeton, and Yale. *General Education in School and College.* Cambridge: Harvard University Press, 1952.

Heely, Allan V. *Why the Private School?* New York: Harper, 1951.

Kraushaar, Otto F. *How the Public Views Nonpublic Schools.* Cambridge: A Study of the American Independent School, 1969.

————. *The Nonpublic School: Patterns in Diversity.* Baltimore, Md.: The Johns Hopkins University Press, 1972.

Prescott, Peter S. *A World of Our Own: Notes on Life and Learning in a Boys' Preparatory School.* New York: Coward-McCann, 1970.